D1562493

Who Is Minding
the Federal Estate?

Who Is Minding the Federal Estate?

Political Management of America's Public Lands

Holly Lippke Fretwell

Published in partnership with Property
and Environment Research Center (PERC)

LEXINGTON BOOKS

A division of
ROWMAN & LITTLEFIELD PUBLISHERS, INC.
Lanham • Boulder • New York • Toronto • Plymouth, UK

LEXINGTON BOOKS

A division of Rowman & Littlefield Publishers, Inc.
A wholly owned subsidiary of The Rowman & Littlefield Publishing Group, Inc.
4501 Forbes Boulevard, Suite 200
Lanham, MD 20706

Estover Road
Plymouth PL6 7PY
United Kingdom

British Library Cataloguing in Publication Information Available

Library of Congress Cataloging-in-Publication Data

Fretwell, Holly Lippke.
  Who is minding the Federal estate? : political management of America's public
lands / Holly Lippke Fretwell.
       p. cm.
  "Published in partnership with Property and Environment Research Center (PERC)"
— t.p.
  Includes bibliographical references and index.
  ISBN-13: 978-0-7391-3101-5 (cloth : alk. paper)
  ISBN-10: 0-7391-3101-X (cloth : alk. paper)
  ISBN-13: 978-0-7391-3102-2 (pbk. : alk. paper)
  ISBN-10: 0-7391-3102-8 (pbk. : alk. paper)
  ISBN-13: 978-0-7391-3103-9 (electronic)
  ISBN-10: 0-7391-3103-6 (electronic)
1. Public lands—United States—Management. 2. Public lands—United
States—Management—History. I. PERC (Bozeman, Mont.) II. Title.
  HD216.F73 2009
  333.10973—dc22   2008050760

Printed in the United States of America

♾ ™ The paper used in this publication meets the minimum requirements of American
National Standard for Information Sciences—Permanence of Paper for Printed Library
Materials, ANSI/NISO Z39.48-1992.

Contents

Figures and Tables

FIGURES

TABLES

Acknowledgments

Beyond the author of any book are numerous contributors, from those who inspire ideas and support staff that help put it all together to family that unwaveringly stand by—all of which have been necessary to make this book possible.

I would like to thank the great staff at PERC that not only helped to motivate this book but also provided insights, scrupulous edits, critical comments, and funding. I would like to extend particular thanks to Terry Anderson for being an incredible mentor and instigating many of the ideas that went into this book. Very special thanks also go to Linda Platts, who spent many hours with me mulling over ideas and carefully editing the chapters bit by bit. I am grateful to Jane Shaw for her final edits to help make each piece of this book concise and to Greg McNamee for his comments.

Many of the ideas for this book came from the people that painstakingly work on the ground in an effort to make our public lands better places. I thank those that were willing to talk openly with me and that provided me with an immense amount of data and information. The creation of this book took generous financial support. I thank the donors that helped fund this project, in particular the Earhart Foundation, the Samuel S. Johnson Foundation, and the Mining & Metallurgical Society of America.

This book is dedicated to the many people that work in public land agencies in hopes they enhance our public lands so that we can continue to enjoy the beautiful landscapes and resources we are blessed with.

Chapter One

History of American Public Lands

The public domain has been a force of profound importance in the nation-
alization and development of the government.

— Frederick Jackson Turner

The largest landowner in the United States is the national government, which controls more than one-fourth of the nation's land area, most of it in the West. This degree of government ownership seems paradoxical in a country founded on principles of individualism, limited government, and private property rights, but the forces affecting land ownership over the past two hundred years can explain the paradox. These include the western territorial expansion of the United States, the long-dominant political power of Eastern interests, and major shifts in public attitudes and expectations, especially at the beginning of the twentieth century.

As a result of this twisting and turning history, the management of federal lands is far from monolithic. Four major agencies control the federal domain, and each has its unique origin, its particular laws and regulations, and its constituents. Private individuals and corporations ranging from multi-national companies that log trees in the national forests to families that visit the Grand Canyon use government-owned land. As Marion Clawson wrote more than two decades ago, "It is precisely in this interface between public ownership and private use of the same lands that the conflicts with federal policy arise and persist" (Clawson 1983, 4).

As the title of this book implies, all is not well on the federal estate. This book will explain the incentives that guide decision-making for this great swath of land under federal control, show why they create conflicts and disappointments, and recommend ways to put into place better incentives.

To choose one typical lament about mismanagement, let us look at the media, which routinely decry the state of our national parks. The *New York Times* wrote in 1999 that "for all its beauty Yellowstone is broken. Hordes of summer tourists and the increasing numbers now visiting in the spring, fall and winter are overwhelming the park's ability to accommodate them properly" (Janofsky 1999). Our forests, too, are the subject of constant policy debates, and even former Forest Service chief Dale Bosworth has said that the agency is suffering from "analysis paralysis." Our grazing lands—which represent the largest single use of federal lands—are beset with conflicts, as environmental groups try to stop livestock grazing and allow it to return to wildlife habitat and ranchers attempt to defend their traditional grazing rights.

Although such issues occasionally hit the headlines and briefly rise into Americans' consciousness, they have not shaken Americans' firm commitment to public land management. Americans believe that their federal agencies are doing a good job. Nurtured by images of Smokey Bear and Woodsy Owl, Americans are convinced that the government is the best possible steward of the land, indeed that only federal agencies can fully conserve the nation's resources for wildlife, recreation, scenic beauty, water quality, and historic value.

When one looks closely at the evidence, however, one finds that this confidence in government management may be misplaced. Many federally managed forests are dense and dying and vulnerable to catastrophic fire. In recent years, wildfires have devastated millions of acres. Rangelands are eroded in spite of ever-stricter government regulations, and America's treasured national parks are rundown and their resources threatened.

Fiscal accountability has eroded, too. Billions of taxpayer dollars are spent every year to manage the federal estate, yet often agencies are unable to account for the money they spend. Although the Government Accountability Office (formerly the General Accounting Office) is not totally unbiased, its reports should cause Americans to seriously question the job that federal land managers are doing. For example:

- Since 1990 the GAO has reported seven times on accountability weaknesses in the Forest Service (GAO 2003a, 2). In 2003 the GAO determined that the Forest Service spent nearly $3 million on improper, wasteful, or questionable purchases (GAO 2003a, 1).
- After two decades of study, the National Park Service still lacks an accurate inventory of resources to develop a reliable estimate of the system's maintenance backlog (GAO 2002b, 1).
- Rapid coal-bed methane gas development on Bureau of Land Management (BLM) land across Wyoming, Montana, North Dakota, Colorado, and New

Mexico has resulted in hundreds of unpermitted coal-bed methane water reservoirs that were unknown to inspectors in the BLM field offices.

Why have the federal land agencies failed to adequately protect the public lands in their care? The answer lies in the political nature of public management. Under current policies, public land managers are beholden to Congress for their budgets. That means they must serve the interests of congressional powers to obtain operating funds, and the results are not necessarily what are best for the resources or for the public. In addition, public ownership tends to encourage interest groups, especially national ones, to battle with local residents and private companies over issues of energy extraction, wildlife habitat, endangered species protection, logging, and even whether or not snowmobiles should be allowed in Yellowstone National Park.

SHAPING A NATION

In this chapter we will look at the history that produced America's federal estate and then more specifically at the development of its key land agencies. The nation's policy with respect to public lands has seesawed dramatically over time. Although the federal government of the thirteen colonies owned no land at first, it soon began to acquire western territories. That era of government expansion was followed by a sharply different era, as the government attempted to empower citizens through private property. Then government acquisition and control returned—and increased. In a sense, the seesawing stopped with the Federal Lands Policy and Management Act of 1976, which mandated that the "public lands be retained in Federal ownership." Today the federal lands are no longer temporary holdings intended for distribution to the people, as they once were, but are permanent responsibilities of the government for the benefit of the people.

The result of this history has been the growth of government agencies whose purpose is to manage this enormous federal estate. This book will focus on the Forest Service (an agency of the Department of Agriculture) and the National Park Service and the Bureau of Land Management (agencies of the Interior Department). The fourth largest land management agency under the federal government, the U.S. Fish and Wildlife Service, had predecessor agencies that focused on research rather than land management. Even with its more recent turn to managing landscapes, its funding and responsibilities are quite different than the other large land management agencies of the U.S. government. The agency is addressed where interesting nuances exist but is not given as much emphasis in this book as are the other agencies.

Operating at the "interface between public ownership and private use of the same lands," as Marion Clawson described federal policy, the land agencies are in the middle of frequent political storms. Each agency's history is distinctive, and each organization is the product of attitudes and political forces that have changed dramatically over the past two hundred years.

As political scientists know, the U.S. government was initially intended to be relatively powerless (a "confederation"), with most decision-making to be conducted by the states. It was also landless. After England recognized the independence of the United States in 1783 and surrendered its claims to the land, individuals or states claimed every acre within the boundaries of the union. The colonies held lands not only within the state boundaries as we now know them, but also westward from the Appalachian Mountains to the Mississippi River.

To boost the newly formed government, the federal government asked states to convey excess lands—lands beyond their formal boundaries—to national ownership. This land would provide a common fund for the benefit of all citizens. One by one, member states began to do this (Gates 1984, 35). These lands transformed the government into a landowner, and the lands became known as the public domain.

As the nation expanded geographically in the nineteenth century, so did the public domain. From the Louisiana Purchase in 1803 to the acquisition of Alaska in 1867, the federal government added 1.7 billion resource-rich acres (Donaldson 1970, 13).

This accumulation of resources created a new set of problems, including great political struggles. Established eastern interests envisioned the land as a revenue generator under federal control. John Quincy Adams described the public domain as an "inexhaustible fund for progressive and unceasing internal improvement" of the nation (Turner 1893, 279). Many Easterners wanted to limit and control the settlement of western land, obtaining revenues from sales but not losing political power to newly developing jurisdictions.

The Land Ordinance of 1785 laid the groundwork for the first legal transfer of land out of the public domain. It required all lands to be surveyed under the rectangular survey system prior to sale. Lands were to be sold at competitive auctions as whole sections of 640 acres (one square mile). The minimum acceptable bid was $1.25 per acre. Private companies conducted most of the land sales until the General Land Office, which later became the Bureau of Land Management, was created in 1812. Revenues generated from land sales reduced the tax burden and the national debt (Nelson 1995, 7; Donaldson 1970, 196). Indeed, by 1836, revenues from land sales made up nearly half of all government receipts (Gates 1984, 37).

Although land sales produced important revenues, there were other purposes for land distribution as well. Transferable land scrip was a reward for military service, often sold at rates below the minimum federal sales price (Nelson 1995, 13). The government gave free land to encourage settlers in Florida, and later in Washington, New Mexico, Kansas, and Nebraska to buffer attacks from Native Americans and enforce the newly formed national boundaries (Clawson 1983, 21). Grants of land to states helped promote the development of schools, transportation routes, and internal improvements to encourage development and settlement.

Over time, the eastern aversion to growing political power in the West increased. In the north, barons of industry feared that western land would lure workers away from their manufacturing facilities. Southern interests feared that westward expansion would increase the number of free states and their eventual supremacy over slave states (Beard and Beard 1960, 245).

But western settlers paid no heed to these fears. They wanted land, and efforts to withhold it were futile. In 1893, historian Frederick Jackson Turner wrote, "The east has always feared the result of an unregulated advance of the frontier, and has tried to check it and guide it. . . . But the attempts to limit the boundaries, to restrict land sales and settlement, and to deprive the West of its share of political power were all in vain" (Turner 1893, 285).

In fact, most people who lived on the frontier land during the first half of the nineteenth century were squatters. Until land was surveyed, it remained under federal ownership, and no one was allowed to obtain title. After survey, even if an individual had improved and developed it, the land could be legally auctioned to another bidder. In this way, the laws were more suited to eastern interests by earning cash receipts that eased taxation than they were to fostering westward expansion.

Westerners often ignored the formal land laws. With few exceptions, land distribution and settlement occurred as people built homes and cultivated the land even though they had no legal right to it. Once it became clear that after land was surveyed, the government could uproot settlers and sell the land to others, local people began to acknowledge preemptive settlement rights. They formed "claim associations" that established who could bid on newly surveyed land at the minimum price. These designations were enforced by threat of harm to those who tried to interfere (Clawson 1983, 21).

LAWS AND CUSTOMS

It took Congress nearly eighty years to adopt laws that began to reflect the realities of the frontier. In 1862, the Homestead Act gave settlers the legal right to claim land they had improved. The Homestead Act was preceded by several preemption acts that gave squatters preference rights for land purchase, in essence expanding what the claim associations had already been doing.

Under the Homestead Act, homesteaders could claim only 160 acres at first, although that figure was later expanded to 640 acres. This was not enough land to sustain a family farming or ranching in the arid West. And the rectangular survey system adopted from the Land Ordinance of 1785 bore no relationship to the geography of the land; rather, it divided land in square miles moving east to west. It differed from the pattern developed over more than a hundred years of land surveying in the colonies, which was irregular and more easily adapted to the landscape (Donaldson 1970, 178). Yet the rectangular survey system was adopted and applied to the frontier, against the recommendation of the geologist and explorer John Wesley Powell that land surveys be respectful of land and water formations.

The Homestead Act conferred permanent ownership to the square tracts of land after five years of continuous occupation and cultivation, thus legitimizing settlement and customary rules by giving the homesteaders and squatters the first right to purchase the land they had cultivated. In the words of President Andrew Johnson, "The lands in the hands of industrious settlers, whose labor creates wealth and contributes to the public resources, are worth more to the United States than if they had been reserved as a solitude for future purchasers" (Donaldson 1970, 349).

But the new law was riddled with problems. Many eastern legislators disapproved of it, because it was seen as expanding the western frontier and diluting eastern political power. Furthermore, the act did not meet the needs of the homesteaders. The acreage limits severely hampered the ability of farmers to sustain themselves on the frontier. Whereas 160 acres were adequate to farm in the East, it was wholly insufficient west of the hundredth meridian. John Wesley Powell recommended as many as 2,560 acres for each settler (Donaldson 1970, vii).

In spite of these flaws, the Homestead Act embodied the view that the public lands should ultimately be transferred to private individuals. But its limitations crippled other uses of the public domain, creating unanticipated chaotic conditions in the future and paving the way for a complete reversal of land disposal policies.

Perhaps the biggest indirect impact of the Homestead Act was on timber. The act favored farmers over all other settlers, requiring agricultural use as a qualification for ownership (Steen 1976, 7). Until 1878, timber production was considered a fraudulent use of the land, even though forests covered great expanses of the West. The Timber and Stone Act of 1878 made forestry a legitimate use of the land, but even then acreage was limited to 160 acres and resale of land was illegal (Libecap and Johnson 1979, 130).

Yet as the country developed economically, wood resources were desperately needed as a fuel source and for the construction of homes and railroads. Motivated by the huge market for timber, businessmen sidestepped the law in pursuit of forestland. Large-scale timber operations were capital-intensive, as railroad lines and heavy equipment were necessary to remove and transport the large-diameter trees. With the 160-acre limitation, a profitable timber operation was impossible. Businessmen resorted to the use of "entrymen" to acquire adjacent parcels that were later combined through prearranged sales. Others, intent on profits through lumbering, ignored land laws entirely. They simply clear-cut swaths on the public domain and then moved on to new territory.

In light of the tremendous demand for timber in the West, it is no surprise that the early land laws proved ineffective. In 1891, an employee of the General Land Office stated that "the laws provide neither adequate method for the protection of the public timber, nor for its disposition in regions where its proper use is imperative. . . . The effect of existing legislation is to force the whole population over large areas to steal the timber" (quoted in Cameron 1928, 113).

A similar independent situation existed on the range. In the West, homesteads of 160 acres provided woefully insufficient pastureland. Even 640 acres,[1] the allowable amount beginning in 1877, was not enough pasturage for a sustainable livestock operation unless irrigation was available. Instead, adjacent unsettled federal lands supplemented private forage. As populations grew, ranchers were forced to compete with each other for grazing opportunities on these federal lands. In many places, overgrazing denuded the land.

As the number of settlers increased, open land became scarce. With no way to claim property rights by creating sufficiently large estates, ranchers were forced to use federal lands to supplement their private range. To avoid the conflict and the resulting excessive use of the common land, herdsmen attempted to better define property rights. For example, ranch operators contracted with outside individuals to file claims on land in the public domain, and then ranchers would buy the land from them at a premium (Anderson and Leal 1997, 29). In this way settlers could purchase the land they needed for a profitable ranch operation, albeit by a method not approved in Washington. Other operators joined stockgrowers' associations, which helped allocate limited water supplies (Anderson and Leal 1991, 28). Such social arrangements helped prevent the overuse of common land, although they were not legally enforceable. Only after social norms were well developed did Congress pass legislation that modified the restrictive land laws and addressed the conditions of the frontier in a realistic manner.

STOPPING THE PLUNDER

Reports of such overgrazing of the public land and the illegal harvest of timber gradually reached the East. From the 1850s forward, the General Land

Office documented theft, misrepresentation, and fraudulent practices. In 1874, the Secretary of Interior reported the "rapid destruction of timber" and requested protective legislation (Steen 1976, 7). Rapacious private interests, it was asserted, were destroying the public domain. A "timber famine" was imminent. In response to these charges, Congress began to withhold some land rather than allow legal settlement on it. In 1891, Congress created the Forest Reserves to ensure future timber supplies for the nation (Libecap and Johnson 1979, 130). Marion Clawson, a key public land scholar, believed, "It was the excesses of the disposal process that led to the permanent reservations in federal ownership of some of the public domain" (Clawson 1983, 27).

In addition to the threats from illegal timber harvest and grazing, farms were springing up everywhere. Crop acreage quadrupled in the twentieth century, as 390 million acres, an area greater than Alaska, were converted from forest to agriculture (MacCleery 1996, 22). Fifteen million acres of forestland were harvested for forest products, compared to less than one million the previous century (MacCleery 1996, 17). In the East, perceptions of settlement were changing. Offended by reports of plunder and fearing the loss of once-abundant resources, easterners questioned the value of channeling some of the nation's unlimited resources into private hands. And many feared a decline of the nation's valuable resources.

The ineffectiveness of western land law and the perception of dwindling resources contributed to the rise of a new approach to government policy that came to be known as "Progressive." Influential leaders began to believe that government could—and must—correct the excesses of the private sector. The government, they believed, could take the long-term view, which the private sector could not, and the government could apply scientific principles in a professional manner, untarnished by the greed they viewed as endemic to the private sector. In this worldview, private individuals were considered outlaws, hastily exploiting the land. Government, on the other hand, was seen as a wise and prudent protector of natural resources.

This move to support public over private conservation marked the beginning of the Progressive Era, a period when government ownership was promoted as the best way to protect and enhance resource values (and which in some ways continues today). The National Park Service, the Forest Service, and, later, the Bureau of Land Management were all created with the belief that the federal government could conserve and steward the nation's most treasured lands better than the private sector.

Yet the reasoning behind the creation of these agencies was flawed. The seeming "crises" of timber theft and overgrazing on public land arose because Congress, dominated by Easterners, had enacted laws unsuited to frontier life. The "crises" also reflected confidence in government that has not withstood the test of time. Policymakers trusted that scientific information would be readily available, that agency personnel would act in the best interest of the land rather than in their own self-interest, and that politicians would favor the broad public interest over the preferences of their constituents.

By that time, however, the nation had been transformed by the disposition of land in the public domain. More than 1.8 billion acres of land, nearly 80 percent of the nation, had once been held in the public domain. While the federal government maintains control of 37 percent of this land, 18 percent was transferred to the states and 45 percent placed into private hands (Clawson 1983, 26).

MANAGEMENT BY THE FEDERAL GOVERNMENT

By the end of the nineteenth century, public land agencies had become permanent managers of the vast federal estates. Disposal was out of the question. In the "interface of private and public interests," each agency developed in its own way, often creating unintended consequences that managers continue to grapple with today. The following discussion will introduce each agency.

The National Park Service

Just as the federal laws limiting land ownership shaped timber and grazing, the formation of the National Park Service reflects the impact of limitations on land ownership. Scholars now recognize that the establishment of Yellowstone National Park, the first in the nation's vast national park system, was not so much due to the vision of farsighted conservationists as it was to the drive for profits by the owners of the Northern Pacific Railroad (Anderson and Leal 1997, 24). They sought to build a railroad across the northern part of the country, providing the only transportation to the famous geysers and spectacular scenery of Yellowstone.

Yet land laws limiting ownership to 640 acres prevented the company from securing enough land to create a reserve that would attract tourists. Rather than attempt to buy the land through fraudulent means, the company decided to try another approach. It funded explorers to research the area, artists to document the spectacular discoveries, and lobbyists in Washington to help convince Congress to set aside Yellowstone as the first national park in 1872. This well-orchestrated effort eventually earned the rail line great profits as the only efficient transportation to the region.

The pattern repeated itself. Several other major western national parks were created as railroad moguls sought to profit from the West's spectacular landscape. Rail companies often lobbied for the parks and held concessions to the parks' original hotels (NPS 1991, 12). The Tacoma Eastern Railroad spurred the creation of Mount Rainier National Park in 1899, in Washington; in 1902 the Southern Pacific Railroad influenced the making of Crater Lake National Park in Oregon; the Santa Fe Railroad was influential in the establishment of Grand Canyon National Monument in 1908, it gained national park status in 1919; and the Great Northern Railroad lobbied for Glacier National Park that was declared in 1910 (Anderson and Leal 1997, 27–28).

Reserving land of national importance began long before the national parks, however (McDaniel 1996, 1). As early as 1790, President Washington authorized the establishment of the District of Columbia for government office buildings, and it is also the site for the Capitol Mall and the Washington Monument. The early nineteenth century saw federal land retained for military purposes, including a forest preserve for navy shipbuilding and mineral springs for presumed health benefits. The first hot springs were set aside in Arkansas in 1832 to promote and protect the supposed health benefits of the hot water—although at some future date the hot springs were supposed to be removed from federal protection (NPS 1991, 15).

California's Yosemite Valley was the first landscape that was legislated for perpetual reservation. The land was granted to the state of California for protection in 1864. The congressional intent was "for public use, resort, and recreation . . . inalienable for all time" (NPS 1991, 10). For similar reasons, Yellowstone was preserved as a "pleasuring ground for the benefit and enjoyment of the people." Because the park's wonders lay in Montana and Wyoming, neither of which was yet a state, the only viable approach was to place the land under federal administration.

Initially, each national park was treated as a separate entity under the jurisdiction of the Secretary of Interior. But without the strength of a unified park system, individual parks could not garner the political support required to ensure their protection. In fact, Yosemite lost a huge and bitter battle to protect existing park resources in 1913 when Congress authorized the city of San Francisco to build a dam and reservoir that flooded the Hetch Hetchy Valley within Yosemite National Park.

To gain both political and societal influence, park proponents worked to establish a national park service. Skillfully lobbying for support from journalists and railroads likely to profit from park tourism, park advocates gained congressional favor. In 1916, Congress authorized the creation of the National Park Service.

The Park Service was to oversee the management of all parks under a dual mandate "to conserve the scenery and the natural and historic objects and wildlife therein and to provide for the enjoyment of the same in such a manner and by such means as will leave them unimpaired for the enjoyment of future generations." Park managers were expected to merge these principles of preservation and utilitarian conservation, ideals so widely divergent in their approach to the natural world that the friendship between John Muir, the noted preservationist, and Gifford Pinchot, the progressive chief of the Forest Service, dissolved in bitter disagreement.

Stephen Mather was appointed to carry out the new Park Service mandates. As an entrepreneur, Mather believed that the most efficient means of running the parks was to charge user fees (McDaniel 1996, 1). In his first report to the Secretary of Interior, Mather stated: "It has been your desire that ultimately the revenues of several parks might be sufficient to cover the costs of their administration and protection and that Congress should only be requested to appropriate funds for their improvement. It appears that at least five parks now have proven earning capacity sufficiently large to make their operation on this basis feasible and practicable" (GAO 1982, 2). The five parks were Yellowstone, Yosemite, Mount Rainier, Sequoia, and General Grant (now part of Kings Canyon/Sequoia).

By 1916, at least seven parks charged auto fees to help meet operational expenditures. Yellowstone charged $10 for a one-year permit, the equivalent of $165 in 2006. Compare that to $40, the actual price of an annual permit in 2006. Mather noted that "no policy of national park management [has] yielded more thoroughly gratifying results than that which guided the admission of motor-driven vehicles to the use of roads of all parks" (Mather 1916, 6).

The receipts from these fees were held in a special account, accessible to the Park Service without congressional appropriation for road maintenance, park development, and administration. Mather considered agency control of the funds important for responsible management and recommended that all parks retain park receipts in the system (Mather 1916, 9).

Park autonomy, however, did not fit the Progressive agenda, and Congress quickly seized control of the purse strings. In 1918, two years after the creation of the National Park Service, legislation was passed ordering all park receipts deposited in the national treasury. The change in financial control was spurred by a dispute regarding the army's role in Yellowstone. The army had been dispatched to the park to protect the wildlife from hunters and the fragile geothermal formations from souvenir-collecting tourists.

When the national parks were ordered to turn over their revenues to the national treasury, political appropriations funded all park activities for the first time. Hence, 1918 marked the beginning of major political meddling in national park affairs. Even the determination of fees became a political function. Congressional debates over appropriate fees have taken place multiple times over the past century. Auto entry fees dropped over time, per person fees were introduced in a few parks, and for nearly four decades national parks were prohibited from charging camping fees (Mackintosh 1983, 11 and 16).

Managers came to view fee collection as a nuisance, and resented spending appropriated funds on fee collection rather than valuable park resources. It would be another fifty years before parks were permitted to retain any portion of the fees, and then only to cover collection expenses (Mackintosh 1983, 47).[2] The link between fees and expenses, visitors and managers was lost. In its place, park managers found themselves directly linked to politicians in Washington, who funded their budgets.

Political interests rarely coincide with the priorities of park managers. One of the reasons why the Park Service has a chronic maintenance backlog is that Congress tends to appropriate funds for new capital projects, even brand new parks, without providing sufficient financial resources to maintain the existing parks and protect their natural resources (Ridenour 1994, 79). Much of the infrastructure for the national parks was built in the 1950s and 1960s, but Congress has provided little for maintenance. New structures and ribbon-cuttings generate far more political capital and, as a result, existing park buildings, sewer systems, electrical systems, and roads are in poor and deteriorating condition. Funds for the occasional crisis or new capital expenditures can always be found, but funding for routine maintenance, repairs, and day-to-day operations is difficult to come by.

Political interference goes beyond maintenance issues to the creation of new national parks of dubious national importance. This tendency goes back to the creation of Platt National Park (now part of Oklahoma's Chickasaw National Recreation Area), a hot springs that was designated as a park in 1906. Historically polluted with sewage and generally unsuitable for a park, the nine-hundred-acre site won park designation through congressional pressure. Following its park designation, there were repeated requests for funds for critical park improvements (Foresta 1984, 11).

Indeed, political pork seems to be a motivating factor in many cases, because congressional representatives have discovered that park creation can bring federal funds to their districts. For example, Lowell National Historical Park in Massachusetts, added to the system in 1978, is a collection of nineteenth-century factories along a canal system; once embedded in the park system, it was restored, helping to revitalize the local economy (NPS 1991, 94). Another is Steamtown National Historic Site in Scranton, Pennsylvania, which houses a collection of old steam rail engines and a roundhouse that is being transformed into a museum. Though of "doubtful" national park stature, says James Ridenour, former director of the National Park Service, it has been a powerful economic development project for the region (Ridenour 1994, 81). Congressional representatives continue to recommend land for inclusion in the national park system for the economic benefit of their constituents.

Despite ongoing problems with maintenance and resource protection, the growth of the Park Service has continued unabated. At its creation in 1916, the system had 14 national parks covering 8 million acres, and 24 national monuments. Eighteen years later, park units had more than doubled to 32 parks covering almost 20 million acres. The number of national monuments had also doubled to 46, which covered less than 1 million acres.

Reorganization in 1933 under National Park Service Director Horace Albright and President Franklin D. Roosevelt further enlarged the system. By presidential decree, all parks and monuments under other departments were reassigned to the National Park Service, adding seventy new units (NPS 1991, 36–41). In the end, the Park Service controlled 114 units on 25.5 million acres. Even that is much smaller than today's system, which includes 380 units and more than 83 million acres.[3]

The number of units worthy of national park status is a subjective determination. What is certain is that even to suggest the removal of units from the system is political suicide. Another certainty under the current management structure is that more parks will be added, and political pet projects will receive more funding than the existing parks in need of maintenance and restoration. From James Ridenour's perspective, federal land management "is a knock-down, drag-out, confrontation with myriad interests" (Ridenour 1994, 13).

The U.S. Forest Service

The story of federal timber management is a "tragedy in which decent people with the best of intentions destroyed what they cared for most," says ecologist and historian Nancy Langston (1995, 6). In hindsight, the national forests have always lacked the independent and scientifically sound stewardship that would sustain them and their wealth of biodiversity.

In the late 1800s, as we have seen, unable to conduct legal logging, some lumbermen practiced cut-and-run forestry. Fraudulent land sales were rampant. Many people came to fear that the nation's forests were being destroyed and that a timber famine was on the horizon. The government seemed to be the one entity that could protect the forests from lawless and rapacious lumbermen.

In reality, timber was not scarce, and the proof lay in the behavior of those who logged the forests. If timber had been scarce, lumbermen would have acquired property rights to be assured of future harvests—even in the small quantities of land that they were allowed to own for timber—and they would have invested in replanting. Instead, it was cheaper to strip the most valuable wood and move on to exploit yet another forest. In addition, tax laws based on the combined value of land and timber encouraged logging to reduce the tax burden (MacCleery 1996, 36).

Politicians did not sit idle as fears mounted and abusive land use proliferated. Rather than allow private owners the option of owning enough land to make timber management profitable, the Progressives of the day opted to rely on government to protect forest resources. The Forest Reserve Act, an eleventh-hour rider that gave the president the right to reserve public domain forestland within the federal estate, was passed in 1891. The act provided the president tremendous powers to ensure the nation a future supply of timber (Steen 1976, 26). It is unlikely that congressional supporters could have predicted the impact the bill would have: In just two years, the president had created 15 reserves covering more than 13 million acres.

The bill's sweeping powers made it possible to establish vast new forest reserves, yet it made no provision for how the land was to be managed (Steen 1976, 28). Administrative duties for the reserves were given to the Department of Interior, which had no conservation or forestry expertise. The Division of Forestry, under the Department of Agriculture, with all the appropriate skills, was left empty-handed. Nonetheless, fourteen more reserves were created, tripling the acres in reserve status.

A more precise definition of the national forest reserves and their role in timber supply was provided by the Forest Service Organic Administration Act, passed in 1897. The federal forests were to supply a continuous flow of timber as well as secure "favorable conditions of water flow." Yet, specific management provisions were still neglected. The Department of Interior only had authority to offer basic timber sales.

By 1905 the forest reserves had been transferred to what was then called the Department of Forestry within the Department of Agriculture, and the reserves became known as the national forests. Gifford Pinchot was appointed the first administrator of what was by then 75 million acres of federal forestland. Pinchot managed the forests for their most productive use, incorporating local information and industry interests (Pinchot 1905, 10). The next decade brought the addition of 88 million acres, boosting total national forest acreage to near 163 million acres (as much as exists in the West today) (FS 2001, 118).

As the scarcity of timber rose, its value increased, and eventually private interests began to pursue long-term timber management. The high cost of obtaining ownership on sufficient acreage for long-term rotational harvest, however, probably postponed such conservation goals for decades. In the meantime, lumbermen migrated, harvesting more virgin forest rather than investing in future productivity, and the federal government became a timberland manager.

Silviculture in the United States

Unfortunately, federal timber management had its own distinctive problems that set the stage for future difficulties. The profession of forestry was new to the United States, and many of the experienced professional foresters of the time, such as Pinchot, had trained in Europe where trees were grown as crops. Forests in Europe had long been managed on a rotational basis where harvest was matched to growth, ensuring sustainable forest products in perpetuity. America's forests were quite different. They were vast and stocked with multiple species of virgin trees in millions of acres that varied widely in climate and topography.

Nonetheless, federal forest managers, using tried European techniques, proposed clearing vast areas of timber in order to plant a more productive and efficient forest. Old growth was considered wasteful and inefficient compared to young and more vigorous trees that could produce a continual supply of timber. In theory, selective harvesting of old growth would reduce competition and increase the growth of the remaining trees, which then could be cut in future cycles. At the end of a full rotation, when all old-growth timber had been removed and replaced with new trees, the forest would contain an equal number of trees in each age class, thus consistently providing full-aged timber for harvest (Langston 1995, 164). At this point, the allowable cut would equal the sustained-yield output, or the annual growth of the forest.

Accordingly, by the 1920s many federal forests in the western mountain region were being cut at an accelerated rate (Langston 1995, 159). In an attempt to liquidate old growth in order to produce a cultivated crop, foresters lost sight of the sustained timber-yield concept that underlay their practices. Harvest in inaccessible areas required substantial investment in rail lines to get the timber out. Such investments demanded large, long-term timber supply contracts with private industry. Rather than wait for high timber prices to stimulate interest in sustainable quantities of timber, federal foresters offered large unsustainable quantities of timber to guarantee a sale.

The Sustained Yield Forest Management Act of 1944 promoted the concept of community stability and further encouraged long-term contracts. The act was meant to ensure a continuous and stable supply for timber-dependent communities. Long-term contracts that guaranteed an annual minimum volume of timber to local mills were granted, at times on 100-year terms (Fedkiw 1996, 45). This practice paralleled the designation of national parks as a way to provide local economic development.

Ironically, the scientific management to adhere to sustained yield forestry was in direct conflict with guarantees of a "sustained level" of harvest. Timber harvest was exceeding what was sustainable for rotational harvest in many regions. The trees would not grow and replace themselves fast enough to continue harvesting at the same level year after year. In the town of Enterprise in the Wallowa Valley, Oregon, 131 million board feet of timber were removed from public land in twelve years beginning in 1915, decimating the accessible timber supply. A mill built in 1914 to support local employment failed in 1928 because there was no longer enough timber to support it (Langston 1995, 160).

The application of European silviculture failed miserably. To determine a sustainable harvest level based on an even-flow rotation, the quantity of standing timber had to be known. But inventorying the forest was costly, and estimates were woefully inadequate. American forests varied greatly, even acre to acre. In addition, because the forests were so old, there was little annual growth.

To cultivate the forest European-style, the decadent old growth had to be removed to allow more vigorous young growth. A formula was derived to determine the allowable cut, equating harvest levels to potential annual growth. But potential growth was another unknown. There was little knowledge of existing timber volume, tree growth, mortality rates, or reproductive capacity.

In the end, the allowable cut was a political compromise. Those desiring heavy harvest had high estimates of potential growth, while those interested in light harvest estimated slow growth. Washington would compromise in between (Langston 1995, 171)—not exactly the scientific management proposed for the reserves.

The Forest Service, which had originally been dedicated to protecting the forests from exploitation, was now itself exploiting the national forests. To produce a regulated forest and a sustained yield of timber, the old-growth forests had to be removed (Fedkiw 1996, 48).

By the 1920s, Forest Service planners knew that current logging practices could not sustain harvest levels for future rotations. Yet the rationale for removing old growth to create more efficient forests was so ingrained that some future losses were accepted as inevitable. On several forests, lucrative contracts led to the construction of such large mills that all the negotiated timber would be harvested in fifteen years if mills were running at capacity. Despite clear evidence of over-harvesting, foresters felt obliged to sustain the mills in the near term (Langston 1995, 190–195). In 1920, timber harvest rates were twice the net growth rate on forestlands. Even the best available scientific information could not overcome the influence of politics on management decisions. Accelerated harvests continued in the 1920s even though foresters knew they were not sustainable.

Over time, conditions changed. Substitutes for timber used as fuel and for construction became available and more long-term forest management was practiced. By the 1950s, forest growth was exceeding timber harvest. The change came about because of rising timber prices. Technological advances introduced steel and concrete as structural substitutes for timber, and coal and oil were used in place of wood for fuel (MacCleery 1996, 47). Higher prices also encouraged greater timber utilization, making more product from one log.

New Problems Arise

As time went on, the Forest Service persisted in its unscientific harvesting, with ramifications that would have an enormous impact in the years ahead. Some areas of excessive harvest and road building were totally unsuited to timber production; the costs of extraction greatly exceeded the timber value. Many areas have been so ravaged that they are known as the "industrial forests" and their managers the "timber beasts." The Bitterroot National Forest in western Montana provides a case in point. It is here that the Forest Service's single-minded approach to timber harvest and its destruction of other forest values first received national exposure.

The Bitterroot National Forest covers steep, rugged mountainous terrain. The slopes are carpeted with ponderosa and lodge pole pine and scattered with high mountain lakes surrounded by snowy peaks. In the 1960s and 1970s, aggressive timber harvests clear-cut large swaths of land and left the slopes scarred by a multitude of crisscrossed logging roads. Called timber mining, these harvests were extractive in nature and conducted in areas with poor prospects for regeneration. The cutover slopes were bulldozed into terraced trenches in order to mechanically plant new seedlings and reduce competition from other vegetation. The regeneration costs alone were estimated to be at least thirty-five times more than the value of the timber (Bolle 1970, 19).

Protests flooded into the agency. Conservationist groups were outraged, but so too were loggers who realized that the excessive harvest would put them out of business in years to come. "The timber stands in our area are being ruined for the next three generations," said Ernie Townsend of Darby, Montana, a third-generation logger (Burk 1970, 11).

More objections to national forest timber plans echoed across the nation. The Multiple-Use and Sustained Yield Act of 1960 had required the Forest Service to provide for multiple uses, including recreation, range, wildlife, and fish, but timber production seemed to be riding roughshod over all other uses. Citizens sought redress in the courts. They argued that a harvest near Wyoming's Bridger Wilderness was poorly planned and destroyed the aesthetic value of the area. In Oregon's Willamette National Forest, demonstrators opposed logging (Burk 1970, 6–7). The Secretary of Agriculture directed a committee to report on the abuses of Forest Service timber harvests in Idaho and Montana.

It was becoming clear that the agency was building timber roads and harvesting without "commensurate consideration" of other forest uses (Burk 1970, 8). The Bitterroot was unquestionably the epitome of single-use management.

Operating from its headquarters in Washington, D.C., the Forest Service was setting resource production goals for land thousands of miles away that could be better managed by decision makers at the local level (see Bolle 1970). A multiple-use approach to natural resources had been designated by legislation and was welcomed by the public, yet timber harvest was the one use directly rewarded by federal appropriations. Forest plans estimated the maximum volume of timber that could be sold without subverting other forest values. Known as the "allowable sales quantity" (ASQ), this measure was intended to be a ceiling, but it became the yearly harvest target.

Many foresters, along with scientists, conservationists, loggers, and other citizens, claimed that the ASQs were ecologically unsustainable and should be reduced by 25 to 50 percent (Wilkinson 1998, 29). Such concerns were largely ignored by Congress, which saw the ASQs as targets and rewarded the Forest Service with funding for all programs when these targets were met. Foresters refusing to achieve the timber quotas dictated by Washington were often harassed and transferred to desk jobs (Wilkinson 1998, 29). Facing such political incentives, most managers worked to meet performance targets regardless of forest productivity or ecological and monetary costs.

As the devastating environmental impacts of these management practices came to light, Congress worked to bring Forest Service management under tighter control. The National Environmental Policy Act (NEPA), passed in 1969, requires federal agencies to report the predicted environmental impacts of proposed actions and possible alternatives. The Forest and Rangeland Renewable Resources Planning Act (1974) and National Forest Management Act (NFMA, 1976) required each unit of the National Forest System to prepare a land and resource management plan after analyzing current and future resource inventories. Furthermore, for the first time, NFMA encouraged public participation in the Forest Service planning process in order to promote greater support and cooperation.

Consensus, however, was not the result. All initial forest plans were appealed at least five times, and forty-nine plans were actually litigated (Fedkiw 1996, 196 and 198). More than a decade after the passage of NFMA, as forest plans were being verified through the appeals process, there were an increasing number of appeals on site-specific projects.

One effect of the new laws was to give higher priority to environmental concerns and reduce the emphasis on timber production. The allowable sales quantity on most forests was reduced, and public input had much greater impact on agency decisions. According to the Forest Service, it has changed its focus from ecologically damaging timber production activities to ecosystem management. On the other hand, the agency's bureaucratic structure and the incentives it creates have not changed.

And in recent years a new crisis has arisen—the crisis of wildfires across the West. Since the great fires of 1910 that burned 3 million acres in Montana and Idaho, wildfire has been treated as though it was a cancer. Yet as early as 1920 there was strong evidence that many forest types were fire-dependent and that fire should have been used as a management tool, not eradicated (Nelson 2000, 99). By the 1960s, the critical role played by fire in forest ecology was indisputable, so much that even national park managers changed their policies, allowing some fires to burn, and setting others.

The public's perception of fire and of the Forest Service, however, did not change. The Smokey Bear ads of the 1940s, telling the public that "only YOU can prevent forest fires," had been one of the most successful advertising campaigns of all time. The ads convinced the American public that forest fires were bad and that forest rangers who put out fires were heroes. To contradict that message and embrace fire—by letting fires burn and even setting controlled fires—was to question the legitimacy of the agency and its claim of scientific management.

It was not until 1979 that the agency recognized the need for fire policy reform and a prescribed burn program, similar to the one that the National Park Service instituted. At the same time, a longstanding policy that called for every fire to be extinguished by 10 a.m. of the following day remained unchanged. As management policies slowly evolved, the ecological systems of many forests were being substantially altered. In the interior West, excessive harvest followed by fire suppression changed once-open savannahs of ponderosa pine into dense fir and pine forests. Competition for sunlight, moisture, and soil nutrients left more than 125 million acres of national forestland susceptible to disease, insect outbreaks, and intense wildfire (GAO 2002a, 1). The altered forest structure together with drought and other weather patterns helped produce catastrophic fire years like 2000 when more than 8 million acres burned, nearly 7 million acres were consumed in 1996 and 2002 by wildfires, and nearly 6 million in 1999.

Today, the Forest Service remains at the center of ongoing controversy. Timber harvest is down 80 percent since its peak in the late 1980s and now accounts for only 5 percent of U.S. timber consumption. Private harvest from southern tree farms as well as wood from abroad makes up the difference. With reduced harvest, less active management, and continuing fire suppression, many forests have grown overly dense. Wildfires are apt to be larger and burn hotter than a hundred years ago. Forests are more vulnerable to insect infestations and disease. Wildlife habitat is lost, water quality is compromised, and property and even lives are endangered.

Active management on many old-growth forests has been halted in an attempt to preserve increasingly rare habitat for certain old-growth species. The buildup of fuels combined with the deteriorating condition of the aging trees could spell disaster for these forests. Chad Oliver, professor of silviculture and forest ecology at the Yale School of Forestry, says, "We have no assurance that forest set-asides will actually grow older. There is a greater probability they will burn up or blow down first" (quoted in Nelson 2000, 55).

Bureau of Land Management

The Bureau of Land Management (BLM), perhaps the least known of the federal land agencies, manages the most federal land—264 million acres plus nearly all federal subsurface rights, or 43 percent of the federal estate. Nearly every kind of land is included in the agency's dominion from wilderness peaks and arid rangelands to wild rivers and oil and mineral reserves. The BLM is best known for its grazing land management, but in addition it produces timber and minerals.

The bureau was created in 1946 when Congress merged the General Land Office, the agency then responsible for federal land disposal, with the Grazing Service, which by that time was allocating federal grazing leases to private ranchers. The BLM assumed administration of all remaining public domain lands and federal subsurface acres while it was also responsible for disposing of these lands. Once containing 1.8 billion acres, the federal government gradually transferred 1.1 billion acres into states and private hands and conveyed more than 350 million acres to other federal land agencies.

The abundance of western rangeland in the late 1800s enabled cattle ranchers and nomadic sheepherders to coexist with little conflict. By the early 1900s, however, more and more settlers were staking claims. The range was still large, but the number of cattle was growing, and homestead laws limited the amount of private acreage. Ranchers who required more land than they could legally homestead had a choice—to reduce herd size, risking the viability of their ranches, or to move the cattle onto public land. In the West, a single cow requires as much as 100 acres to survive for one year, and in the Southwest it can be as high as 500 acres (Nelson 1995, 17).

As we have seen, ranchers initially combined homesteaded property with adjacent federal land. Over time, more ranchers, more cattle, and more nomadic sheepherders meant competition for federal grazing lands and eventually these common lands became denuded as livestock competed for every blade of grass (see also Anderson and Hill 2004). Increased competition for forage developed into range wars among the livestock owners who could not privately hold enough land to sustain their herds.

The creation of customary rights and collaborative groups began to resolve the conflicts, however. Ranchers on the Great Plains defined range rights, which were respected by their neighbors, to ensure exclusive use of the land. Stockmen in Montana and Wyoming formed cooperative associations to administer use of private, state, and federal rangeland. The Montana territorial legislature passed a law defining grazing rights on the federal domain (Anderson and Leal 2001, 30). None of these arrangements were legally enforceable under federal land laws.

As with past legislation, customary rules provided the framework for eventual congressional legislation. In this case it was the Taylor Grazing Act of 1934, which defined public land grazing rights. The act authorized a new Division of Grazing (later the Grazing Service) to create rules for livestock use of federal lands. By 1936, 142 million acres of the public domain were included in grazing districts, with preference given to those with nearby private land.

The act recognized forage for livestock as the highest valued use of the land, "pending final disposal." It was unclear what the final disposition was to be, but meanwhile few other uses were permitted in grazing districts, with the exception of mineral and oil exploration.

When the BLM was created, it assumed responsibility for vast amounts of land as well as all the conflicting land laws and regulations that went along with the public domain. For thirty years, the agency attempted to fulfill a vaguely defined mission of land disposal and land retention along with providing grazing rights and mineral rights. In 1976, Congress passed the Federal Lands Policy and Management Act (FLPMA). This law confirmed that federal lands would be retained in federal ownership and repealed many of the early land laws. Much like legislation regarding the Forest Service, it directed the BLM to provide for multiple uses by adhering to rigid planning guidelines.

Today the BLM manages 264 million acres of public land mostly in the West. It provides for nearly 12,000 grazing leases—but also hosts more than 50 million visitors a year. Previously overlooked in favor of national forests and national parks, BLM lands have been discovered by the public as some of America's last best places. In trying to manage for multiple uses, the agency is pressured by groups of every persuasion from ranchers to rock climbers. BLM management decisions are tempered by competition among special-interest groups.

The Fish and Wildlife Service

The Fish and Wildlife Service has a mission "to conserve, protect, and enhance fish, wildlife, plants, and their habitats for the continuing benefit of the American people" (DOI 2007). It is responsible for the management of 96 million acres, 545 refuges, and 37 wetlands management districts. It operates sixty-nine National Fish Hatcheries, seven Fish Technology Centers, and nine Fish Health Centers. The Fish and Wildlife Service has evolved into an agency responsible for the management of a network of land and water across the nation, in addition to a multitude of other conservation activities including brokering funds from the federal level to state wildlife agencies, monitoring, listing, and enhancing habitat for threatened and endangered species and enforcing endangered species legislation, management and law enforcement responsibilities for migratory birds, and monitoring for early detection of avian influenza. Initially, however, the drive to create the bureaus that now make up the Fish and Wildlife Service was to obtain research to assist commercial production in fisheries and agriculture.

Unlike the creation of the other federal land agencies, which came about in response to the changing land uses across the nation, the Fish and Wildlife Service was created by joining two research-focused bureaus. The first, the U.S. Fish Commission, was established in 1871 as a government agency to study declining numbers of commercial fish stocks. Later titled the Bureau of Fisheries, it was also responsible for regulating the harvest of various marine species. What later became known as the Bureau of Biological Survey is the second predecessor, established in 1885. Initially designated to research the relationship between birds and commercial agriculture, the Bureau soon became responsible for wildlife research, predator and rodent control, wildlife regulation, and refuge management. The merger of the two bureaus took place in 1940 when the negotiation of international treaties and agreements was added to its already varied responsibilities.

Similar to the other land agencies, part of the impetus for such a conservation agency was the lack of well-defined property rights. Prior to the pilgrimage of Europeans to North America, Native Americans had ownership systems over wildlife with enforceable rights to hunting and fishing territories (Lueck 1995, 3). These rules were difficult to enforce as Europeans moved into the region, and management of wildlife fell to the states upon their creation.

The laws of the day allowed private ownership of wildlife only if it was dead. Fencing in wildlife was illegal, but killing granted rights to it. Although laws limiting harvest and sale evolved over time, around 1900 the populations of a number of desirable game species were declining. President Theodore Roosevelt, a conservationist and a sportsman, responded by setting aside acreage for bird and game habitat, some of which became a part of today's wildlife refuge system. The first was Pelican Island Bird Refuge, 5.5 acres in Florida placed under federal control in 1903. Its purpose was to protect nongame birds from poachers that were collecting and selling the plumes and other feathers.

By the end of his term, Roosevelt had set aside fifty-two areas for the protection of wildlife. But it was not until 1966, under the National Wildlife Refuge System Administration Act, that comprehensive legislation addressed the management of these wildlife refuges.

In this era the agency's focus changed form research to conservation. In 1970 the agency's commercial research functions were assigned to the Department of Commerce, narrowing the agency's goal to wildlife conservation. In 1993 most other research functions were transferred to the National Biological Survey and ultimately to the Biological Research Division of the U.S. Geological Survey.

Today's Fish and Wildlife Service is responsible for managing and enhancing habitat for wildlife, plants, and some fish species, on the public lands and in partnership with private landowners, in United States and abroad. About 20 percent of the agency budget goes to management of the wildlife refuges and 10 percent is strictly for threatened and endangered species conservation. The remainder is split among the agency's many other conservation responsibilities.

CONCLUSION: THE EVOLUTION OF PUBLIC LAND POLICY

The paradigm guiding federal land management has shifted from disposition of land for revenues to retention of land for conservation. Restrained by eastern perceptions in the nineteenth century, the disposal process never adequately accommodated the needs of western settlers. Cultural norms evolved on the frontier, taking the place of federal laws, but they were viewed as fraudulent and corrupt by influential figures in the East. Rather than allowing the settlers to establish mutually agreed-upon rules for land use, the government interceded and introduced the reforms espoused by Progressives—especially the decision to stop selling land.

But the politicians created agencies that provided public land managers with incentives that the politicians didn't anticipate and didn't understand. Federal forest managers, for example, were no better at conserving the landscape than the cut-and-run lumbermen who preceded them. In an attempt to satisfy constituents, they allowed timber to be harvested even where other values exceeded that of timber production. Such incentive problems plague the land agencies today.

The government attempted to solve the public land problems, many of which it had created, by replacing a restricted market approach with government management. But just as political forces earlier led to laws that ignored the needs on the frontier, political forces continue to steer federal management. The result has been conflict, indecision, and lack of accountability, problems that this book will analyze in some depth.

NOTES

1. Desert Land Act of 1877.

2. Public Law 92–347.

3. National Parks Conservation Association: About national parks. http://www
.npca.org/about_npca/park_system/default.asp. Cited May 11, 2006.

Chapter Two

Federal Agencies Lose Money

The most visible sign of problems with public land management is the substantial losses that federal land management agencies incur every year. The land management agencies of the United States—the Bureau of Land management (BLM), the Fish and Wildlife Service, the Forest Service, and the National Park Service—oversee an estate of 614 million acres rich in timber, minerals, livestock forage, wildlife habitat, recreation sites, and natural beauty and scenic grandeur. The value of this land is estimated at more than $150 billion (O'Toole 1997, 5), though the true value is incalculable. Expenses and revenues can be calculated but missing from the equation are the intrinsic and other values not being measured by the market. Each year, management costs for these public lands reach billions of dollars, and yet there is no return to the taxpayers on this investment. In fact, the government loses more than half of each dollar spent.[1]

At first glance, these losses might seem acceptable. Governments are not expected to make a profit. But, just like many private landowners, these agencies supply goods and services to corporations and individuals and charge them money. Indeed, the Forest Service was formed to ensure that the nation would always have enough forests to supply the nation's timber needs, and at times in the past, the Forest Service covered more than its costs. Today, however, all four agencies lose money, unnecessarily burdening the American taxpayer.

At the root of the agencies' financial problems is the dominance of political management. Generally, Congress funds the budgets of the Fish and Wildlife Service, the Forest Service, the Bureau of Land Management, and the National Park Service. This gives land managers an incentive to respond to politicians more than they respond to public users of national forests, parks, and rangelands. A closer look at the budget process will show a number of flaws that come from this system. These include political interference, disincentives for cost reduction, and, ultimately, public land managers who have little real control over the resources in their care.

FUNDING FOR FEDERAL AGENCIES

The land management agencies earn money from sales of natural resources such as timber and minerals or from fees from users. But most of this money is sent back to the general treasury rather than retained by the agency or onsite. As a result, no connection exists between money spent and money earned. In a typical business, the customers' payments determine how much money the company can spend. In the case of public land management, however, agencies' budgets have little relationship to their revenues from "customers." Controlling costs to make sure that they do not exceed revenues is an abstract concept rather than a fiscal necessity.

The consequences of this condition are illustrated in the National Park Service in the early 1990s. Until 1993, fee revenues earned in the national parks reverted to Washington, D.C. The parks themselves received no direct benefit from collecting fees,[2] and the cost of collecting fees—such as the cost of posting rangers at park gates—had to be paid out of the parks' general appropriations. Managers were, in effect, punished for collecting fees. After press reports showing that many parks were failing to collect fees, Congress passed legislation in 1993 to help cover collection costs. The law allowed up to 15 percent of fee collections to be retained onsite to cover the costs of collection. This addressed one problem, but the larger problem of making a connection between visitors' demand and a park's budget was still missing.

In some cases where revenues do come from customers, the interaction between congressional appropriations and revenues further complicate land management. In the case of timber sales, for example, a Forest Service manager relies on appropriated dollars to prepare the sale—that is, to identify the parcel of forest that will be sold for logging and to conduct the activities included in the planning process and environmental analysis. Once the sale is complete, about half the proceeds are retained at the forest unit to be used for reforestation and other resource improvements, while the rest is returned to Washington.

Keeping half the proceeds reduces the dominance of the congressional budget process, but this arrangement has an impact that also affects incentives. Because a significant amount of money comes from logging, managers have an incentive to encourage harvest over other uses in order to fund improvements. At the same time, because all the costs of sale preparation are covered by congressional appropriations, the system provides no incentive to control the costs of sale preparation. This lack of incentive to control costs contributes to below-cost timber sales.

Similar situations, or disconnects, exist in other land management agencies. Like the Forest Service, most BLM expenses are covered by appropriated dollars. The BLM retains a portion of grazing fees for rangeland improvement, so grazing gains precedence over other land uses.

Managers have little discretion as to how agency money is spent. Even with the revenues such as the forest restoration fees, the monies are directed to select accounts for specified uses or uses specified by federal laws. Money appropriated by Congress is earmarked for a particular purpose. That purpose may be politically motivated, such as spurring local economic development or pleasing certain constituent groups. In one case, Montana's congressional delegation earmarked $3 million to restore two backcountry chalets in Glacier National Park (*USA Today* December 15, 1997). The chalets were used by less than 1 percent of park visitors, who must hike or ski into the chalets between July and September. A few Montanans, organized as Save the Chalets, had lobbied for the restoration and were fortunate to catch the attention of the Montana congressional delegates, because they were unable to raise their own funds for the project. One of the restoration's major expenses was for toilets—a $1 million privy. This is a self-composting unit (with a solar-powered generator to ensure proper composting in freezing weather, although the chalet is not open during winter months). Since installation, the unit has proven ineffective at self-composting and the waste must now be flown out via helicopter. This privy was built even though Glacier's superintendent had set as his top priorities visitor center improvement and road repair—projects that went unfunded. Such political earmarking comes at the expense of resource stewardship and facilities maintenance.

Another aspect of federal land management budgeting that discourages cost control is the "use it or lose it" policy endemic in bureaucratic organizations. Any portion of the budget not spent at the end of the fiscal year is returned to the treasury. Rarely can the money be rolled over into the next year. Additionally, the next year's budget is based on the money spent in the previous year. Thus, a manager who tries to save some money for the future in effect reduces the size of the following year's budget. Rather than have an incentive to reel in costs, managers are encouraged to spend all of their budget appropriations in a single year to ensure that next year's budget does not shrink. Spending sprees at the end of the fiscal year are commonplace. Yellowstone National Park typically spends 70 to 90 percent of its budget, excluding overhead, in the last two weeks of the fiscal year.[3] There is no reason to think that other agencies are different.

THE COST OF MANAGEMENT

The budgeting process has resulted in annual management costs that continue to rise over time. Despite the public's impression that appropriations are tight, operating budgets for the four federal land agencies have increased 270 percent faster than inflation since 1962.

Perhaps it is easier to grasp the growth in costs when they are viewed acre by acre. In 1965, management costs per acre were less than $5. By 2002, costs had more than tripled to an inflation-adjusted $16 per acre (see figure 2.1). The problem is that these increases do not get translated into more effective management.

The public image of tight budgets does apply to funding for infrastructure and major maintenance. In the national parks, appropriations for construction and maintenance have fluctuated during the past four decades, but the average annual increase is less than 1 percent, even though the number of facilities continues to rise (see figure 2.2).

Imagine a grand old hotel with a staff to run it, but next to nothing for maintenance and improvements. That is essentially how Congress funds land management. Consequently, the agencies have tremendous maintenance backlogs and deteriorating infrastructure. The Forest Service has $5 billion in deferred maintenance projects (*Federal Parks & Recreation* 1999, 1), which is more than matched by the National Park Service (Vincent 2002). Congress funds bureaucratic growth rather than investing in the long-term stewardship of national lands and facilities.

Figure 2.1.   Federal Land Management Costs per Acre
Source: OMB 2003; also see footnote 1.

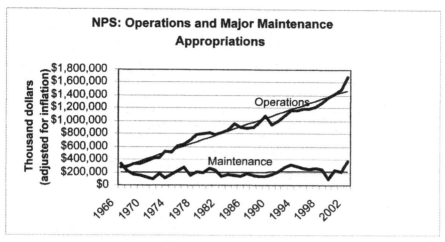

Figure 2.2. NPS Operating vs. Maintenance Budget
Source: OMB 2003; NPS Budget Justification FY 2003.

This short-term outlook is the result of politicians' efforts to garner votes. Elected officials want the political support that comes from taking credit for new facilities and new parks. Championing support for maintenance and repairs is not nearly as appealing or glamorous as ribbon-cutting—so these essential areas are often neglected.

When a crisis arises—one often stemming from deferred maintenance—congressional representatives race to gain credit for allocating funds to the neglected resource. It was not until Yellowstone's aging sewer system spewed raw sewage into the park's trout streams that Congress came to its rescue. The Going-to-the-Sun Highway in Glacier National Park closed several times due to safety concerns before Congress approved funding to examine the need for road renovations. Multiple summers of exacerbating wildfires on federal forestlands finally prompted funding for wildfire risk-reduction activities. Although funds are short for day-to-day maintenance, dollars flow unimpeded when high-profile cases can reap political rewards. Rather than investing capital in long-term maintenance and stewardship, Congress directs funds to short-term projects with high visibility or constituent interest (see Leal and Fretwell 1997; Stroup and Goodman 1992). Given these political incentives, Congress often favors capital projects over managers' down-to-earth requests, and pork-barrel projects like the Glacier outhouse are funneled into the home districts of elected officials.

In some cases, the incentives facing park managers themselves lead to decisions that are not in the interest of either the taxpayer or the park visitor.

Yellowstone's Norris campground is a case in point. In 1996, when Yellowstone Park managers were running short of funds, they decided to close the
park's popular Norris campground and two park museums. Managers were
then able to use the $70,000 it cost to run these facilities for other park re-
sources. Yet the campground fees alone had brought in $116,000 in 1995—far
more than the costs. But because these revenues were returned to the general
treasury, the managers did not benefit from them. They did, however, bear
the cost of operating the facilities. To cut their costs, closure made sense, but
it was a loss to taxpayers and to park visitors (Fretwell 1999b, 9).

The closure was more than just a cost savings; it was also a political ploy.
Shutting down the popular campground brought an onslaught of complaints
from the public that predictably attracted the attention of Congress. This
tactic, called the Washington Monument strategy, has been used before by
the Park Service. According to Interior Department lore, at one time, in order
to obtain more funds, park officials threatened to reduce visitor hours at the
monument, the most popular site on the Capitol Mall. Not surprisingly, Congress increased the monument's budget the next year.

The same strategy won Yellowstone an additional $1.8 million in the
following year's budget.[4] By closing the popular Norris campgrounds and
museum, the Park Service irritated enough people that Congress paid attention. But this kind of activity perpetuates the uneven and erratic relationship
with Congress. Incentives to maximize the value of assets or keep costs low
are still lacking.

So, largely because Congress is in the driver's seat and because its interests
may differ dramatically from those of on-the-ground managers, land agencies
lose a lot of money. Between 1998 and 2001, the BLM and Forest Service
lost on average more than $2.7 billion each year. In other words, these two
agencies earned just fifty cents for every dollar that they spent. The National
Park Service generated just twelve cents for every dollar spent.[5] The three
agencies combined experienced a total loss of $4.4 billion, producing a bal-
ance sheet that in the private sector would have sent shareholders fleeing.
Taxpayers, however, do not have that option.

STATE TRUST MANAGEMENT OF PUBLIC LANDS

Not all government land agencies are money-losers, and we can learn a great
deal by scrutinizing state land agencies that have goals similar to the federal
land agencies. States often sell timber, lease livestock forage, and provide
recreational and conservation opportunities. But many earn a profit doing so.
Although states may not offer ideal public land management, they provide a
benchmark against which federal management can be measured.

Beginning with the admission of Ohio into the Union in 1802, every western state has been granted federal public domain lands for the benefit of public schools, colleges, state institutions, and other internal improvements. The states were provided one or two sections of every township. The Enabling Act accepting each state into the union defines the grant purpose, restrictions, and limitations. Current law in each state now provides that those lands be held in trust.

Today twenty-two states are responsible for federally granted lands. Although the management forms have evolved for more than a hundred years, a clear purpose weaves a common thread through them. Each trust is managed by a public entity to provide financial support for schools and other specified beneficiaries. Each trust is required to provide financial benefits forever into the future. These trust requirements make them uniquely different from private and other public land management.

Although they are considered public lands, state trust lands have first and foremost the goal of providing funds for the specified beneficiaries—typically the public schools and other state institutions. Like other trusts, they are expected to provide fiduciary responsibility, which, as defined by common law, means that revenues to the beneficiaries are expected to exceed costs for every trust activity. The trusts can provide benefits to the public so long as the trust is compensated for doing so.

Thus, the defining difference between federal and state land agencies is the requirement for the states to generate revenues in excess of their expenses. They have a bottom line, unlike federal agencies, and are mandated to generate revenues for the benefit of public schools. Furthermore, the beneficiaries—school administrators, teachers, parents, and students—provide oversight and have standing to sue trust managers for financial losses or unreasonable expenses.

Although the trusts are expected to make a profit, the perpetual nature of the state land-grant trusts requires the equal consideration of benefits today and in the future. This was emphasized in a Montana Supreme Court case, *Thompson v. Babcock*. The court concluded that preserving the trust properties for ongoing income potential had priority over maximizing immediate trust income. Thus, stewardship to maintain the long-term productivity of the land is part of the trusts' fiduciary responsibility.

The tables and figures that follow illustrate that state land agencies are controlling costs and generating revenues from trust lands, while federal land agencies lose money. Between 1998 and 2001, the BLM lost on average six cents for every dollar spent, the Forest Service lost on average seventy-seven cents for every dollar spent, and the NPS lost eighty-eight cents for every dollar spent. During the same period, thirteen western eighty-eight earned a combined average of $9.32 for every dollar spent managing trust lands (see table 2.1).[6]

Table 2.1. Land Management: Federal vs. State

	Revenues ($ Million)	Expenses ($ Million)	Revenue/Dollar Spent
Forest Service	767.8	3,384.1	0.23
BLM	1,680.5	1,781.5	0.94
NPS	226.3	1,925.2	0.12
Average State Trust Lands	68.9	9.5	9.32

Note: 1998–2001 average, in 2000 dollars. State Trust Figures are based on the average for state-managed lands, including Arizona, Colorado, Idaho, Montana, New Mexico, North Dakota, Oklahoma, Utah, Oregon, South Dakota, Utah, Wisconsin, and Wyoming.

Sources: BLMD, FSD, and NPSD as cited in note 1; STLD as cited in note 3.

Not only do the federal land agencies earn less than the state trust lands, they outspend state agencies by a wide margin (see figure 2.3). The Forest Service spends nearly thirteen times more per acre than the average state trust agency, and the National Park Service spends seventeen times more. Even the BLM, controlling 264 million surface acres and 300 million subsurface acres, outspends the average state trust more than two to one.

DISAPPEARING FEDERAL DOLLARS

Comparisons with state trust lands shed some light on federal agencies. The federal agencies themselves do not have adequate information about their

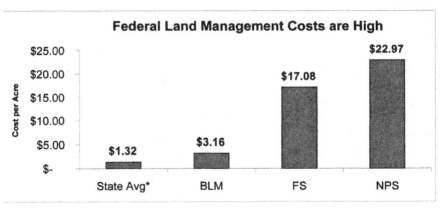

Figure 2.3. Federal vs. State Costs per Acre

Note: 1998–2001 average, in 2000 dollars. State Trust Figures are based on the average for state-managed lands, including Arizona, Colorado, Idaho, Montana, New Mexico, North Dakota, Oklahoma, Oregon, South Dakota, Wisconsin, Utah, and Wyoming.

Source: BLMD, FSD, and NPSD as cited in note 1; STLD as cited in note 3.

own costs and revenues to reveal their efficiency or lack of it. Lack of fiscal accountability by the Forest Service and the Bureau of Land Management makes accurate and meaningful data collection virtually impossible. The Government Accountability Office (GAO, formerly the General Accounting Office), reporting on "audits, surveys, investigations, and evaluations of Federal programs,"[7] has repeatedly criticized the reliability of the accounting practices of the Forest Service (GAO 1998b).

During the past decade, the Forest Service's Inspector General, whose goal is to ensure that legal procedure is followed, found Forest Service financial statements inadequate in eight out of ten audits (OIG 2002). For example, in fiscal year 1995, the Forest Service could not account for $215 million of its $3.4 billion operating budget (GAO 1998a, 5). In 2000, inadequate accounting led to a $274 million violation of firefighting expenses (OIG 2002). A chief reason why neither the Forest Service nor the BLM can provide consistently accurate accounting of their spending is that they track only budget allocations, not actual expenditures. Any budget manager knows that budgeted expenditures can differ significantly from actual spending.

Data for the financial analysis in this book was accumulated from a variety of sources for the years 1999 through 2001. In 1999, the Forest Service adopted a new accounting system in an attempt to better measure ecosystem outputs such as ecosystem assessment and planning, ecosystem conservation, and public services and uses. The new ecosystem outputs are difficult to compare with categories designated under the previous accounting system making it impossible to accurately track comparable expenses into the future. It is for that reason, the figures in this analysis reflect the years 1998–2001. Regardless of the specific methods used, the Forest Service and BLM continue to account for their actions as planned, rather than as performed. Actual expenditures are still largely unaccounted for.

HIGH COSTS OF FEDERAL LAND MANAGEMENT

One thing that is evident, even with the limited information available, is that inefficiency is contributing to the high costs of federal land management. A telling indicator of efficiency is the relative number of employees per acre. The bureaucracy-laden federal agencies have on average ten times as many employees per acre as state land agencies. Per million acres under management, the National Park Service has 237 employees, the Forest Service has 159 employees, the BLM 19 employees, and the states average just 13.[8]

The Forest Service claims its management inefficiencies are amplified by excessive paperwork required by law. Planning and assessment costs exceed one-quarter of a billion dollars annually. This constitutes 40 percent of the total workload at the national forest level. The Forest Service estimates that as much as $100 million is spent on unnecessary planning that could be better used for critical forest restoration projects or other on the ground management activities (FS 2002, 5).

Federal agencies also fall down in comparison to the states in terms of revenues generated per employee. The states generate four times more revenue per average employee than the BLM, fourteen times more than the Forest Service, and forty-eight times more than the National Park Service. In fact, Forest Service and National Park Service salaries on average exceed revenues earned per employee (see figure 2.4).

The inefficiencies of federal land management are further demonstrated when their activities are compared to the same activities carried out by state agencies. Comparing state and federal land agencies by activity provides a way to measure relative fiscal performance for these different land uses among the agencies. The following discussion will cover timber, grazing, minerals, and recreation.

Timber

Federal timber sales generate the most revenues from surface land, but these revenues are depleted by disproportionately high expenditures. The federal land agencies lose nearly half of every dollar spent for timber management. It is often assumed that the cause of the money lost on timber sales is subsi-

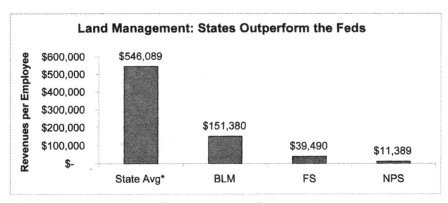

Figure 2.4.   Revenues per Employee, State vs. Fed.

Note: 1998–2001 average, in 2000 dollars. State Trust Figures are based on the average for state-managed lands, including Arizona, Colorado, Idaho, Montana, North Dakota, Oklahoma, Oregon, South Dakota, Utah, and Wyoming.

Source: BLMD, FSD, and NPSD as cited in note 1; STLD as cited in note 3.

dies to timber purchasers, but the evidence does not support this contention. Providing subsidies to timber companies is unlikely when federal timber sales take place in an open public auction, as most do.[9] Although the agency often builds or pays for timber roads, the dollars bid for purchase of the timber take into account these expected agency expenditures.[10]

A closer examination shows that the inefficiencies in federal timber management can explain below-cost sales. Federal timber sales result in both high costs and low revenues, while state timber sales produce substantial revenues as well as lower costs. A state-by-state analysis in western timber-producing regions shows that state trust lands generate over five dollars for every dollar spent, while the federal agencies lose money (see table 2.2).

The cost of federal timber harvests is startling. Between 1998 and 2001, the BLM spent $658 per thousand board feet (mbf) of harvested timber and the Forest Service spent about one-third of that, an average $238 per mbf. The states spent just one-third of that, an average $79 per mbf. (In general, it takes 11 mbf to build a 1,900 square foot house.)

A more precise comparison can be drawn on highly productive timber lands in Oregon where the BLM spent $734 per mbf of harvested timber, while on state land in the same region, Oregon spent a mere $119. With no requirement to cover the bottom line, the federal agencies have little incentive to control costs.

In addition to costing a lot, timber harvested from federal lands generates little return. The average revenue from federal timber is $220 per mbf. The states generated over $350 per mbf. In Oregon, state trust lands generated an average of $523 per mbf, including timber from the less-productive eastern region. The BLM generated only $326 per mbf on its productive lands in western Oregon (see figure 2.5).

A detailed study by Donald R. Leal comparing federal and state timber programs shows the discrepancies in costs and revenues (Leal 1995). By comparing adjacent forests of similar type and productivity, Leal determined that while Montana national forest timber sales lost nearly half of every dollar spent on timber management, the Montana state trust lands generated

Table 2.2. Timber: Federal vs. State   (Mil 2000 $)

	Revenues	Expenses	Revenue/Dollar Spent
Forest Service	410.6	630.5	.64
BLM	47.8	99.3	.48
State Trust Lands	78.9	11.0	5.61

Note: 1998–2001 average, in 2000 dollars. State Trust figures are based on the average for state-managed lands, including Idaho, Montana, Oregon, and Washington.

Sources: BLMD and FSD as cited in note 1; STLD as cited in note 3.

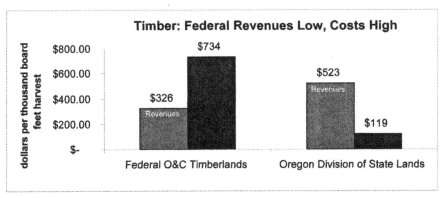

Figure 2.5. Timber Return
Note: 1998–2001 average, in 2000 dollars
Source: BLMD and FSD as cited in note 1; STLD as cited in note 3.

more than two dollars for every dollar spent. Additionally, Montana laws require states to abide by environmental regulations similar to those required of federal timber management. In fact, an independent audit showed that the state did a better job of protecting the watershed after harvest than the federal agency (Leal 1995, 6 and 11).

An independent study completed at the University of Montana shows similar results. It concluded that national forest timber management costs per mbf exceeded the costs of the Idaho and Montana state trust agencies. The study also pointed out that on federal lands, the cost for road construction, reconstruction, and related personnel greatly surpassed state costs for similar work (Keegan et al. 1996).

State land agencies must meet environmental mandates that are similar to the federal National Environmental Policy Act (Mortimer 1999). The Montana Environmental Policy Act, the Idaho Forest Practices Act, and Oregon regulations, which are among the strictest in the nation, all guide their respective state land agencies. Once again the states come out on top according to independent audits of forestry best-management practices. The states do an equivalent or better job than the federal agencies at protecting the soil and water resources on timber harvest sites (MDNRC 2006, 2; IDHW 1997).

Another sign of good forest management by the states is certification by the Forest Stewardship Council. Certification marks good stewardship and compliance with environmental, social, and economic standards. Many state forests have been certified, including those in New York, Minnesota, and Pennsylvania. Washington is in the process of certification assessment, and other states are considering it.[11]

States are also quicker to respond to natural disasters affecting forestlands. Following a fire, blowdown, or insect infestation, the value of timber rapidly declines. After the 2000 Bitterroot fires in western Montana, the state took immediate action to remove the dead wood from the forest floor. By March 2001, the state had removed 22 million board feet of dead timber, generating about $200 per thousand board feet.[12] The Forest Service, however, was tied in a legal quagmire—it took a year and half to get on the ground. Facing threats of litigation and appeals, the Forest Service reached a court settlement that reduced restoration harvest by 66 percent.[13] By summer 2002, only 8 million board feet had been removed from the federal portion of the Bitterroot. The value of the federal timber had declined by about 75 percent, a result of blue rot and insect holes bored clear through the small-diameter trees.[14] Delayed action by federal agencies reduces timber revenues.

As long as federal land agencies have no requirement to cover their expenses, they are not likely to do so. From 1974 to 1978, more than one-half of the national forests did not recover the costs of timber management and reforestation from timber sales (Fedkiw 1996, 220). More than twenty-five years later, that trend continues. According to Forest Service records, in fiscal year 1998, the forest timber-sale program lost $125.9 million. Excluding harvest for stewardship or personal use, more than 80 percent of the commercial timber sales on national forests produced receipts that were less than the cost of timber management (FS 1998d, 113–134).

Timber is one area where managers have an incentive to generate revenues. The Forest Service is able to retain about half of its timber receipts, which are deposited into the Knutson-Vandenberg (K-V) fund for restoration, reforestation, and other activities in the sale area such as tree thinning, wildlife enhancement, and recreation improvements. As a result, managers have an incentive to increase harvest in order to obtain revenues (O'Toole 1988, 183)—but no incentive to keep the costs down, because the costs are paid for with appropriated dollars.

Certainly, the Forest Service has emphasized timber harvest over other activities. As public preferences have changed over time, revealing greater concern about protecting watersheds and limiting logging, Congress has passed rigorous environmental regulations. NEPA and NFMA were largely the result of the public uproar of the late 1960s in response to excessive timber harvesting in the Bitterroot, Monongahela, and other national forests (see chapter 1).

To date, federal land managers still do not have the ability to generate revenues sufficient to cover the costs of land management, and increased regulation has driven the cost of timber management still higher. Growing numbers of court suits by environmentalists eager to stop logging have driven up costs as well. In 1988, Forest Service appeals and litigation costs alone exceeded $5.5 million. It is estimated that between 1980 and 1995, appeals, court decisions, regulations, and statutes increased the costs of timber sale preparation by 25 to 33 percent (Fedkiw 1996, 212).

Grazing

Grazing also comes at a great cost to federal taxpayers. Both the Forest Service and the BLM have grazing programs, although the BLM has far more land in this use. Between 1998 and 2001, the two agencies lost more than eighty cents of every dollar spent on rangeland management. At the same time, the states earned an average of nearly three dollars for every dollar spent (see table 2.3).

Again the culprits are both high costs and low revenues. Since 1996, federal grazing fees per animal unit month (AUM, the amount of forage needed for one cow and calf; one horse; or five sheep or goats for one month) have remained near the minimum allowable fee of $1.35. On state lands, fees start at between $2 and $7 per AUM and increase relative to the forage quality and regional market rates (see figure 2.6). While the states generate nearly $2 for every AUM, the federal agencies lose nearly $5 per AUM.

Similar to timber management, federal land managers are encouraged to generate revenues for management activities, but they are not encouraged to address costs. As with timber harvests, a portion of grazing fees is retained by the agency for restoration and land improvement activities. This provides an incentive to give grazing priority over nongrazing uses such as wildlife habitat. Costs are paid through appropriations from tax dollars and out of fee retention.

Recognizing that their revenues must exceed costs, states have begun to adjust to the changing values for range use. Historically, most rangeland

Table 2.3. Grazing: Federal vs. State

	(Mil 2000 $)		
	Revenues	*Expenses*	*Revenue/Dollar Spent*
Forest Service	6.7	45.3	0.16
BLM	14.0	76.9	0.19
State Trust Lands	13.2	4.4	2.87

Note: 1998–2001 average, in 2000 dollars. State Trust Figures are based on the average grazing revenue only but all agriculture-related expenditures for state-managed lands, including Idaho, Montana, New Mexico, Oregon, and Utah.

Sources: BLMD and FSD as cited in note 1; STLD as cited in note 3.

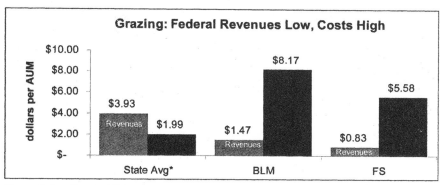

Figure 2.6. Grazing Return

Note: 1998–2001 average, in 2000 dollars. State Trust Figures are based on the average grazing revenues only but all agriculture-related expenditures for stage-managed lands, including Idaho, Montana, New Mexico, Oregon, and Utah.

Source: BLMD and FSD as cited in note 1; STLD as cited in note 3.

was seen as valuable for only one use — livestock grazing. Today, managers recognize that the range provides a multitude of values in addition to grazing livestock, such as protecting water quality and providing wildlife habitat and recreation. While state grazing fees have long reflected costs, now states are beginning to look for higher revenues where possible from other land uses.

Arizona and New Mexico allow nongrazing interests such as environmental and conservation groups to bid against grazers for use of the land. Other states lease land to private groups that conserve the land in the way they deem most appropriate. Thus the growing interest in replacing livestock with wildlife still allows the states to earn revenues that cover their costs.

Minerals

Minerals are the only commodity from federal lands that generate a positive return.[15] From 1998 to 2001, mineral production earned about five dollars for every dollar spent (see table 2.4). While these earnings appear to be substantial, they are a fraction of what could be earned. States that produce minerals from public lands earn an average of more than forty-five dollars for every dollar spent.

Comparing mineral management expenses for state and federal agencies, however, can be deceiving. Many states assign duties such as enforcement of mining environmental regulations and reclamation rules, bond requirements, and onsite inspections to other state offices. The result is that mineral management costs for state agencies are underestimated.

Table 2.4. Minerals: Federal vs. State

| | (Mil 2000 $) | | |
	Revenues	Expenses	Revenue/Dollar Spent
All Federal Lands	1716.0	284.9	5.11
State Trust Lands*	41.4	0.5	46.79

Note: 1998–2001 average, in 2000 dollars. State Trust Figures are the average for states, including Idaho, Montana, New Mexico, Oklahoma, Oregon, and Utah.

Sources: BLMD and FSD as cited in note 1; STLD as cited in note 3.

Even so, evidence from a 1997 GAO report including all expense data for states supports the lower costs generally reported by state agencies. The report showed that New Mexico and Wyoming still earn more than twice what the federal government earns. New Mexico generated sixteen dollars for every dollar spent, and Wyoming earned twelve dollars.

Recreation

Touted as the fastest-growing use of federal lands, recreation loses more money than any other activity on the federal lands. It costs the BLM and Forest Service $295 million for recreation management above earnings (see table 2.5). Most visitors to these federal lands pay little or nothing for recreational opportunities, so the taxpayers pick up most of the tab for management.

Figures on per-visitor costs to federal lands have been distorted in the past by gross exaggerations in the number of visitors. At one time, people who sped through the national forests on highways were counted as forest visitors, bringing the total visits to national forests in 1998 to almost a billion (*Oregonian*, November 15, 2001). Since then, the National Visitor Use Monitoring Project has instituted new procedures for the Forest Service, showing visits for 2000 at around 209 million—a conservative figure compared to earlier estimates.

Nonetheless, even with these more accurate figures, earnings from recreation come to just pennies per visitor. The calculated return is 22 cents per

Table 2.5. Recreation: Federal vs. State

| | (Mil 2000 $) | | |
	Revenues	Expenses	Revenue/Dollar Spent
Forest Service	69.6	318.6	0.22
BLM	7.5	53.8	0.14
Montana Trust Lands	.5	.05	9.81

Note: 1998–2001 average, in 2000 dollars.

Sources: BLMD and FSD as cited in note 1; STLD as cited in note 3.

Figure 2.7. Recreation Return
Note: 1998–2001 average, in 2000 dollars
Source: BLMD and FSD as cited in note 1.

person engaging in recreation in the national forests. The average earning from visitors to BLM lands is fourteen cents, though this may as much as double when this agency too incorporates the new methodology from the monitoring project. The National Park Service tends to have better estimates based on actual users and they do somewhat better, generating as much as seventy-nine cents per visitor (see figure 2.7).[16]

In addition to revealing how little the public pays for access to millions of acres of federal lands, these figures show that for just $1.50 a day, BLM and Forest Service recreation users could pay their own way. If they did, the $295 million tab to taxpayers could be eliminated. A $1.50 fee is very different from pricing people off public lands, a fear expressed by many environmental and outdoor recreation groups. Furthermore, a fee of $9 per person would cover Yellowstone National Park's entire operating budget. This potential to generate critical revenues through reasonable to modest fees has been largely untapped.

Recreation is a money-losing proposition because the costs greatly exceed the revenues collected. The Forest Service and BLM lose an average of eighty-two cents of every dollar spent on recreation management. Starting in 1996, however, the Fee Demonstration Program began to change the incentives for federal land agencies. The program allowed managers to collect recreational fees, like entrance and parking fees, and keep up to 80 percent of the revenues to cover their costs and initiate new projects. The program has helped reduce losses for recreation management by $50 million since the 1994–1996 period (Fretwell 1998, 12).

More realistic fees also create a front-line response from land managers that benefits recreation users. Managers are able to put the fees to work immediately by making onsite decisions to improve recreational facilities and resources or to reduce recreational impacts on the land. With the clear incentives provided by fees, managers have been able to improve upkeep, provide more recreation opportunities, protect visitor health and safety, enhance wildlife habitat, and care for the resources. Under the Federal Lands Recreation Enhancement Act of 2004, Congress extended the program for at least ten years. Lengthening the program ensures managers long-term funding for recreation management and encourages investment in fee collection apparatus such as entry gates and self-pay fee boxes.

Although the Fee Demonstration Program encourages managers to raise revenues and spend them on the land and resources, it fails to provide an incentive to control costs with the monies appropriated by Congress. And congressional appropriations still represent a major portion of their budgets. As long as operations are funded mostly by Congress, managers can ignore the economic realities of balancing costs and benefits.

Another drawback to the program is the tendency for managers to give recreation priority over other land uses such as protecting wildlife habitat and water quality, which do not earn fees. A similar problem occurred with the K-V funds collected from timber sales, which spurred Forest Service managers to emphasize timber harvest. Nonetheless, the recreation revenues provide managers with flexibility to respond to resource priorities over political desires and they provide a signal about the desires of resource users.

Fire

Management problems and financial problems are closely intertwined in the area that has captured great public attention and created the greatest headaches for the Forest Service and the BLM: wildfire. As the next chapter will discuss, wildfire is the biggest deterrent to good stewardship. It is also tremendously expensive. In the last decade, wildfires have become the fastest-growing expense for federal land management agencies. Between 1977 and 1992, costs for large fires were just in excess of $3.5 billion (adjusted for inflation to 2000 dollars).[17] In a single season, the summer of 2000, the cost of fighting and suppressing fires reached $1.6 billion (Arno and Allison-Bunnell 2002, 7). Annual fire suppression costs have exceeded $1 billion at least 3 times since the 2000 fires (USDA 2006, i). These expenditures do not include all of the losses incurred—the loss of homes and lives, the degradation of water quality, the destruction of wildlife habitat, and other forest values (see figure 2.8).

When wildfire-suppression costs exceed the funds appropriated for wildland fire management, federal agencies borrow from other accounts to cover

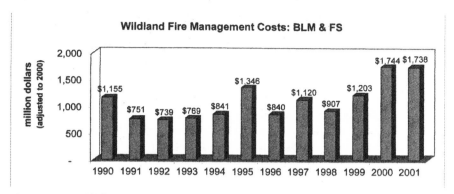

Figure 2.8. Wildfire Management Costs

Source: OMB outlays. Available at www.whitehouse.gov/omb/budget/fy2003/db.html.

the expenditures. At the end of the season, when all the fires have been snuffed out, Congress fills the financial void by reimbursing the agencies for firefighting expenses. The total firefighting bill is paid with tax dollars, most from emergency funds, not the Forest Service budget. In the meantime, while many other agency projects go unfunded, expenditures on fighting wildfire go unchecked. Since 1908, Congress has provided an open checkbook to cover fire suppression expenses (Arno and Allison-Bunnell 2002, 17). Following the devastation of the 2000 fires, agencies were rewarded with increased funding of $1.8 billion—most for firefighting forces and equipment (Arno and Allison-Bunnell 2002, 170).

Firefighting costs have grown 8 percent each year from World War II to the present (Arno and Allison-Bunnell 2002, 23). Yet average acreage burned has also increased. It was at the insistence of the Office of Management and Budget in 1979 that the Forest Service began to alter the fire exclusion campaign to include fuel reduction in the forests (Arno and Allison-Bunnell 2002, 23).

Still, financial incentives to fight fire are strong. At an annual cost reaching $1 billion, battling summer blazes provides reliable seasonal work and is a politically popular economic boost to remote communities where firefighting efforts are based. A dry season in Montana's Lolo National Forest, for example, can generate fire suppression expenditures more than ten times those required in a wet season (Matthews 1997). Firefighters attached to the Bureau of Indian Affairs can earn more than $10,000 during a bad fire summer, which in turn qualifies them to collect unemployment benefits for the rest of the year (Matthews 1997).

Fighting large wildfires costs an average of $570 per acre, often with little success.[18] This does not include the additional costs associated with the destruction of wildlife habitat, soil erosion, water quality degradation, and forest restoration. The Forest Service projects an average increase in firefighting expenses of $19 million a year into the near future (Nelson 1999, 16).

In contrast, fire *prevention* projects must be paid from the annually appropriated budget. Congress allots just $1.25 per acre for fire prevention on Forest Service land that is considered at high risk to wildfire. Little can be accomplished for that price, but for $40 to $50 per acre the Forest Service could manage the land to prevent some inferno-type fires (Glickman 1997, 19), using controlled burns, thinning, and other silviculture techniques. Despite these benefits, the multimillion-dollar emergency fund for firefighting provided by Congress is a powerful incentive to the Forest Service to make firefighting, not fire prevention, a high priority.

As an alternative to fire suppression, active forest management including prescribed fire and mechanical treatments can help moderate fire intensity, but the land manager must tolerate more risks than many are willing to. As the 2000 wildfires in Los Alamos showed, even prescribed fire can be difficult to control. This prescribed fire blew out of control and consumed over 45,000 acres and destroyed about 220 homes. In fact, successful fire-risk management may increase the number of fires, though lower in intensity, as the natural fire process is reintroduced into the system. If a prescribed burn goes awry, the manager is held accountable. If smoke affects the health of citizens or obscures the scenery, the manager is at fault.

Forest treatments must abide by a myriad of regulations that often inhibit managers from accomplishing even simple tasks. The rules require an environmental analysis, public input, and assurances that proposed actions do not conflict with water and air quality. Rules that were intended for the protection of the environment can actually hamper restoration efforts. Carbon dioxide emissions from a prescribed fire may exceed air quality limits, though wildfire emissions would dwarf such pollutants.

While restoration treatments are thoroughly planned and scrutinized for any environmental impacts, wildfires burn under emergency conditions with little time to weigh the costs and benefits of any action. "Frenzied efforts" to control Idaho's Clear Creek Fire in 2000 on the Salmon-Challis National Forest, for example, resulted in a bulldozed fire break 200 feet wide and nearly 200 miles long costing $71 million. Ultimately the effort and the funds were wasted, as fall rains dampened and slowed the blaze before it ever reached the monstrous firebreak (Arno and Allison-Bunnell 2002, 171). After a fire, the environmental impacts of the actual firefighting effort are barely evaluated.

Managing forests to control the risks of wildfire is still not widespread. Many people still view wildfires as uncontrollable acts of nature. Furthermore, fuel-reduction efforts, whether using fire or mechanical means, are labor-intensive for the managers, come with high costs, high risks, and political ramifications, all of which quickly doom many projects.

Another complicating factor is the formula used for funding fuel-reduction projects. Funds are allocated based on the number of acres to be treated, rather than focusing on the areas at highest risk (GAO 2000a, 6). Much like national park managers who find themselves renovating backcountry chalets rather than repairing roads, forest managers respond to political incentives. To please Congress and win larger appropriations, they are motivated to treat as many acres as possible. Understandably, they select areas that are easily accessible and require less treatment. This encourages the treatment of areas in the wildland-urban interface, whether they need it or not. But it ignores more remote areas at extreme risk that may also have highly valued amenities such as provision of drinking water and wildlife habitat. Managers have an incentive to maximize acreage restored so that it can be reported to Congress.

The culture of federal land agencies has long supported the view that fires must be suppressed at all costs. Politicians thousands of miles away in Washington with constituents whose homes could be reduced to cinders support fire suppression and are unlikely to be persuaded that funds would be better spent on active forest management. Changing the way government deals with wildfire will not occur quickly or easily.

FISCAL TRENDS

Pressure from environmental organizations has shifted the focus of federal land managers away from commodity production (production of timber, livestock forage, and minerals) toward more environmental management. This move has not solved the fundamental fiscal problems of the agencies and their lack of accountability. Slight increases in budgets for recreation and amenity protection confirm a change in the trend of spending. But, lacking a well-understood definition of ecosystems and their management or agreement on the goals of environmental management, the agencies have no objective measure for the effectiveness of the change in spending.

Nonetheless, spending trends are now more focused on amenities than commodities. The total budget for the Forest Service and BLM increased 8 percent more than inflation between the mid-1980s and the 1998 to 2001 period, while commodity outputs were falling.[19] Many expenditures once considered part of the timber sales management budget have been shifted to the ecosystem assessment and planning budget. The use of funds is the same, but the name has changed. Curtailing commodity production does not reduce or eliminate land-management costs; it merely transfers expenses to other management areas, much of which is a mere adjustment in accounting.

It is arguable whether declining commodity production is environmentally beneficial, but it is certain that the decline provides little financial advantage. National forest timber harvests have declined more than 70 percent since 1980, but timber sale expenditures have declined by only 56 percent. The cost per board foot has risen 57 percent. Expenditures for federal rangeland management have actually increased by 20 percent since the mid-1980s even though authorized AUMs have declined by 7 percent.[20] Overall, the cost has risen from around $3 to nearly $7 per AUM.[21]

At the same time, funds for resource management have increased. Recreational funding for the Forest Service and BLM increased 110 percent from the mid 1980s (NAS 1986, 1987) to the 1998 to 2001 period. Expenditures for other resource amenities including wildlife and fisheries, soil, water, and air, ecosystem planning, and watershed restoration have shown smaller increases, rising from 10 percent of the agency budgets in 1985 and 1986 to an average 12 percent in the 1998 to 2001 period, but adding a total of $167 million to the tab. The fire budget has seen the greatest increase, more than doubling, a rise from 12 percent of agency budgets in the mid-1980s to 27 percent in the recent period (see figure 2.9).

Increasingly, money earmarked for conservation management is directed toward land acquisition rather than infrastructure and maintenance. Funding for BLM and Forest Service land acquisitions nearly doubled to $200 million between the mid-1980s and the 1998–2001 period. During that same time, outlays for capital improvements and maintenance for facilities and roads dropped 20 percent.

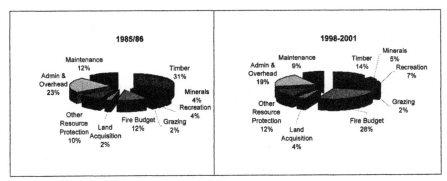

Figure 2.9.   Forest Service Budget Allocation
Note: 1998–2001 average, in 2000 dollars
Source: BLMD and FSD as cited in note 1; F85/6 as cited in note 14.

Measuring the performance of these conservation expenditures is difficult because the inventory of resources on federal lands is grossly inadequate. No benchmark exists from which to measure changes. Although budgets have been altered and funds shifted toward conservation practices, such shifts are no guarantee of improved stewardship, nor is there any quantifiable evidence that stewardship has improved.

CONCLUSION: FEDERAL LAND MANAGEMENT COSTS ARE HIGH, REVENUES LOW

The land management agencies have little or no fiscal accountability. Congress controls most of the purse strings. A series of federal laws and congressional earmarks mandate specific expenditures and allocations of funds, regardless of whether they are suited to the goals of the site where they are to be spent. The result has been mounting costs and low revenues, along with little knowledge of whether the goals of the American people are being met.

In contrast, the states that manage lands under land-grant trusts have a clear and singular goal: to provide revenues to support public schools and other public institutions. With this incentive to maximize long-term value, they are able to keep costs low while delivering a superior environmental and economic performance. The states provide a valuable benchmark against which federal lands can be compared.

NOTES

1. In this document the following data sources shall be referred to as BLM: BLM expenditure and receipt data for the period 1998 to 2001 are from *Budget Justifications* (BLM 1998–2003); *Public Land Statistics* (BLM 1998–2001); BLM FOIA request of November 29, 2001; telephone and written communication with Lori Castaneda, BLM accountant, Denver; onshore minerals costs and receipts are from Minerals Management Service, available at www.mrm.mms.gov/stats/pdfdocs/coll_lc.pdf; and telephone and written communication with James Stockbridge, Budget Officer, Minerals, Revenue Management, Mineral Management Service, Denver.

The following data sources shall be hereinafter referred to as FSD: Forest Service expenditure and receipt data for the 1998 to 2001 period are from *1999 Budget Explanatory Notes* (FS 1999); *Budget Justifications* (FS 2000–2002); written communication with William Helin, Program & Budget Analysis Staff, Forest Service, Washington, D.C.; and written communication with Richard Thornburgh, Program & Budget Analysis Staff, Forest Service, Washington, D.C.

The following data sources shall be hereinafter referred to as NPSD: National Park Service expenditure and receipt data are from Budget Request (NPS 1999–2002); *Recreational Fee Demonstration Program Report to Congress* (USDI & USDA 2001).

2. Several legislative reforms have allowed revenues be deposited into a special treasury account available for appropriation to the parks. Congress and the Office of Management and Budget, however, have used these accounts as an offset to lower appropriations (see Mackintosh 1983).

3. Personal communication, Don Striker, former comptroller, Yellowstone National Park, October 5, 2001.

4. Personal communication, Don Striker, Comptroller, Yellowstone National Park, October 1, 1999.

5. See note 1.

6. In this document the following data sources shall be referred to as STLD: Arizona State Land Department (1998–2001); Colorado State Board of Land Commissioners (1999–2001); written communication with Jim Ball, Public Information Officer, Idaho Department of State Lands, Boise; written communication with Connie Dark, Fiscal Officer, Montana Department of Natural Resources and Conservation, Trust Land Management Division, Helena; New Mexico State Land Office (1998–2001); written communication with Della Gutierrez, Deputy Director, New Mexico State Land Office, Santa Fe; written communication with Gary Presley, Commissioner, North Dakota Land Department, Bismarck; written communication with Keith Kuhlman, Real Estate Management, State of Oklahoma Commissioners of the Land Office, Oklahoma City; telephone and written communication with John Lily, Assistant Director of Policy and Planning, Oregon Division of State Lands, Salem; written communication with Bryce Healy, Deputy Commissioner South Dakota Office of the Commissioner, Pierre; written communication with Dave Hebertson, Public Relations, State of Utah Trust Lands, Salt Lake City; Washington Department of Natural Resources (1998–2001); written communication with Michael Paus, District Office Administrator, Board of Commissioners of Public Lands, Wisconsin, Madison; and Wyoming Board of Land Commissioners (1998–2001).

7. GAO Reports Main page. Available at http://www.gpoaccess.gov/gaoreports/index.html.

8. Includes surface and subsurface acreage. The state average includes Arizona, Colorado, Idaho, Montana, North Dakota, Oklahoma, Utah, South Dakota, and Wyoming.

9. Collusion among bidders would reduce the timber price. See Baldwin, Marshall, and Richard 1997.

10. See also Jackson 1987, explaining other differences between national and state timber stumpage prices.

11. It is not clear whether federal lands are eligible for certification.

12. Electronic transmission from Jon Hayes, December 2, 2002. Montana Department of Natural Resources and Conservation, Helena.

13. www.fs.fed.us/r1/bitterroot/recovery/bar_page/facts.htm. Some research also indicates that post-fire harvest may not be desirable; see Donato, et. al. 2006.

14. Gordy Sanders, Pyramid Lumber, Telephone communication, May 21, 2002, Seeley Lake, Montana.

15. For purposes here, federal minerals include only onshore minerals on federal lands. Total costs and revenues are as reported by the Forest Service, BLM, and Minerals Management Service.

16. It is assumed that national park visitor counts are more accurate than other federal land agencies by use of limited entry and exit ways, permits, and fees.

17. Written communication with Dennis Lynch, Department of Forest Sciences, Colorado State University, October 7, 2002.

18. Ibid.

19. In this document the following data sources shall be referred to as F85/6: BLM expenditure data for 1986 are provided by *Audubon Wildlife Report 1987* (NAS 1987, 16); and Forest Service expenditure data for 1985 are provided by *Audubon Wildlife Report 1986* (NAS 1986, 34).

20. Rangeland expenditures for the 1980s are an average of 1983 BLM rangeland expenditures and 1985 Forest Service grazing expenses, as provided in Audubon 1986, pages 34 and 513.

21. 1986 BLM grazing expenditures were used from the 1987 Audubon Wildlife Report, page 16.

Chapter Three

Steward Problems

In 1997, President Clinton convened a summit meeting to address environmental problems facing Lake Tahoe and the surrounding area. On their way to the meeting, congressmen drove along a road that dropped out of the high Sierras of California into the basin below. Abruptly, the scenery changed from healthy green forests to forests mottled with sickly brown stands of dead or dying trees. It appeared as if someone had drawn an imaginary line across the landscape and arbitrarily decided to kill the trees on one side while nourishing those on the opposite side. "This forest looks like hell," commented Senator Richard Bryan of Nevada later, at a session on forest health.[1]

The aging and diseased property was not a neglected forest owned by private industry. It was part of the Lake Tahoe Basin Management Unit of the Forest Service, and to a large extent the forest looks the same today as it did then.

The Tahoe Basin forests are composed primarily of fir, which grew up after early settlers and miners razed the Jeffrey and ponderosa pines (WCSHF 1997, 3). The Forest Service has managed the Tahoe Basin forests since 1899. They were originally known as the Tahoe Basin Forest Reserve. The Forest Service has followed policies of strict fire suppression and, later, restrictions on logging in the basin. This combination of forces has caused the fir to grow in stands far denser than under natural conditions of moderate intensity fires. It is estimated that parts of the forest are 82 percent denser today than in 1928 (WCSHF 1997, 3). The trees compete with each other for moisture, sunlight, and soil nutrients making them more susceptible to insect infestation and wildfire. In addition, following a decade of drought, bark beetles and disease have ravaged these stands, killing more than 80 percent of the trees (WCSHF 1997, 4).

In jeopardy is Lake Tahoe, known as one of the clearest, deepest lakes in the world. Its beauty has drawn sixty thousand residents to the basin area and attracts 3.5 million visitors every year. The pristine quality of the lake is being threatened by erosion and pollution. Studies show that it is losing nearly a foot in clarity each year. The management of the Lake Tahoe National Forest has put at risk the very qualities it was supposed to preserve, the integrity of the forest and the clarity of the lake below, as environmental regulations delay management actions and restrict timber harvests and forest treatments.

How could this happen? That is what the congressmen wondered when they saw the forest in 1997, and it is what many people wonder about today. Throughout the public land agencies the problems are not just financial, as we saw in chapter 2, but they are ecological.

The four principal federal land management agencies—the Forest Service, the Bureau of Land Management, the National Park Service, and the Fish and Wildlife Service—all operate under general guidelines that call for the protection of water, air, and soil and the preservation of wilderness, landscape beauty, and biodiversity (FS 1998c). By using scientific management as opposed to economically based management geared to produce revenues or benefits for the owners, the agencies are expected to provide the best possible stewardship for the resources.

But in many cases, the opposite has occurred, as illustrated by Lake Tahoe. The Forest Service is not alone. Other agencies suffer severe criticism as well. For example, the National Parks Conservation Association says of the national parks, "Wildlife species are disappearing. Important museum artifacts are not being preserved. Irreplaceable historic structures are crumbling."[2] The grazing practices of the Bureau of Land Management are also frequently criticized, although there is no generally accepted condition for what grazing land should look like. The majority of scientists surveyed at the Fish and Wildlife Service felt they did not have the resources to "adequately perform [the agency's] environmental mission."[3]

Part of the difficulty facing land managers comes from the lack of clearly defined goals. Unlike private companies, which seek to earn a profit, public agencies have many goals. The Forest Service and the Bureau of Land Management are mandated by Congress to provide for multiple uses—for the hunter and the hiker, for the logger and the four-wheeler.[4] The National Park Service is charged with conserving scenery, natural and historic objects, and wildlife.[5] The Fish and Wildlife Service has a seemingly dominant goal to provide for the conservation of fish and wildlife species, but they too are providing for the enjoyment of the people for hunting, fishing, and other forms of recreation.

So many competing goals virtually invite special interests into the policy-making arena. Timber companies battle with environmentalists over commercial harvests in the national forests, and ranchers defend their grazing leases against those who consider cattle grazing an abuse of public lands. "Cattle free," "predator friendly," "no fee, keep it free," and "zero harvest" are slogans that various groups unite behind in their quest to place their visions of land management on the federal landscape.

Complicating the Forest Service's problems is the forest planning process. Although the goal of planning is good stewardship, the complexity of the process has tended to paralyze the agency. The Forest Service is required to complete detailed plans to guide the management of each national forest every ten to fifteen years. Because extensive public participation is required, and because interest groups are deeply divided over the goals of the Forest Service, the first round of plans took nearly two decades and $250 million to develop. And these plans have been shattered by events—such as sudden, devastating fires.

For example, in 2000, massive fires burned hundreds of thousands of acres outside Missoula, Montana. Forest plans clearly do not prepare for such a catastrophe. It took two years and numerous court hearings to reach a court-ordered settlement on what to do next. By 2004, only 40 percent of the restoration work was completed, conflict between environmental groups and Forest Service managers continued, and allocated restoration funds had been siphoned to cover subsequent year firefighting costs (Devlin 2004).

Most forest plans are now due for revision, but in spite of spending tens of millions of dollars annually, the Forest Service has found it difficult to develop plans that are "legally defensible, scientifically credible and able to sustain the forests' resources" (GAO 2000c, 1). Historically, forest plans have not been adapted to the structural changes in the forest, the growing scientific understanding of them, or the increasing human demands on them. Forest plans are often inflexible and unresponsive to changing conditions.

While federal land managers respond to political incentives and pressures, private land managers and some state land agencies are motivated by economics and to some extent are shielded from political pressures. Their experience shows that it is possible to produce landscapes with abundant wildlife habitat, clear streams, and aesthetic beauty while also generating revenues. They are clearly getting different, and often better, results—a fact that might surprise some critics.[6]

In this chapter, we will focus on a key problem facing the Forest Service, the ecological impact of fire suppression. We will also examine how other managers—specifically, state and private owners—address stewardship and then look at some initiatives used on federal lands that mimic some of the incentives of private and state managers.

FIRE SUPPRESSION

The paramount problem of the Forest Service is dealing with the results of decades of fire suppression, including its effects on wildlife and endangered species. As discussed in the previous chapter, the Forest Service has had a policy of suppressing fires for nearly a century. That policy has led to enormous firefighting costs incurred by the Forest Service. It has had a tremendous impact on the ecology of the forests as well.

Fires were once intentionally set by Indians to clear brush and encourage the growth of forage. Lightning fires were once common summer occurrences in the West. Frequent fire, every five or more years, kept the ground clear and encouraged the growth of stately fire-resistant pines. Low-altitude pine forests took on a savanna-like appearance dominated by large, thick-barked, widely spaced trees.

At the start of the twentieth century, fire suppression began. At the same time old pine was removed to supply timber products and the savannas became home to a multitude of new saplings. But without fire, dense, spindly trees grew up filling the once open savannahs. The removal of fire has allowed underbrush to proliferate and fire-prone and shade-tolerant trees to flourish and multiply. The result is a forest unlike the forests that existed in previous centuries. Satellite images of these forestlands show unusually large areas of dense growth with no openings or clearings. As trees struggle to survive, competing for sunlight, moisture, and nutrients, the forest is more susceptible to intense fire, insects, and disease than the forests of the past.

Fire suppression has had the greatest impact on areas historically sustained by high fire frequency, especially in the Inland West, where fires were typical every five to twenty-five years. Many of these forests have not burned now for a hundred years and more. Drought and a spark are all that is needed to bring a new, more deadly fire to the landscape; a fire that reaches the crowns of the trees and burns the forest to the ground. It has been broadly estimated that 90 to 200 million acres of federal land are at high risk of such catastrophic fire (FS 2003a, 14), and that the greatest problems exist on public lands (Clark and Sampson 1995, 2).

In the Wallowa-Whitman and Umatilla National Forests of eastern Oregon and Washington, for example, six million acres of trees are dead and dying. The forests are located in the Blue Mountains, which derived their name from the constant haze of wildfire smoke that once engulfed them each summer.

The frequent, small fires cleared the understory, allowing the stately, fire-resistant ponderosa pines to flourish.

Wagon trains traveling west along the Oregon Trail rolled easily between the widely spaced trees of the open forest landscape. Journals of the time consistently remark on the immense trees standing within open savannas. One early traveler, while on the east slope of the Cascade Range in Washington, noted, "There is so little underbrush in these forests that a wagon may be drawn through them without difficulty. . . . The level terraces, covered everywhere with good grass and shaded by fine symmetrical trees of great size whose open light foliage the sun's rays penetrate with agreeable mildness, give to these forests the appearance of an immense ornamental park" (Bonnicksen 2000, 349).

The fire suppression in these forests beginning in the early twentieth century was followed by logging in the late 1940s. Much of the pine overstory was logged, removing the large, healthy, and mostly fire-resistant trees. A series of insect infestations followed. By the 1980s, the dense nature of the fir stands made them ideal habitat for the western spruce budworm. The infestation spread rapidly, sometimes reaching epidemic proportions. Realizing the seriousness of the problem, federal managers sought to remove infested trees. Speedy timber removal in some areas could have disrupted the infestation, but it often took five to ten years to complete the regulatory process necessary to remove a single piece of wood from the forest (Committee on Agriculture 1997). Today, these mountains are known for their gray ghosts, trees that are dead and dying from the spruce budworm (Peterson 1992, 4).

In other regions, intense wildfires have already destroyed fish and wildlife. In the summer of 1992, east of Boise, Idaho, a crown fire that raced across the landscape destroyed a rare population of bull trout, taking not just timber resources but also every living thing in its path while spewing tons of carbon dioxide into the air. The fire scorched the stream down to the bedrock, wiping out the entire fish population.

In eastern Oregon, the endangered spring chinook salmon makes its home in the Grand Ronde River. In 1989, a raging inferno known as the Tanner Gulch Fire triggered a debris torrent thirty-six miles upstream, wiping out the entire population of salmon. Dr. Victor Kaczynski, a freshwater biologist working on salmon recovery strategies, says, "No single forest practice—not timber harvesting, nor road building—can compare with the damage wildfires are inflicting on fish and fish habitat" (*Evergreen Magazine* 1994–1995, 53).

Charred mountain slopes and stream banks devoid of vegetation lead to increased spring runoff and lower summer water volumes. The low water and lack of forest cover translate into higher water temperatures in the summer and colder water temperatures in the winter. Fish populations suffer from these extremes, and increased erosion chokes spawning beds with sediment. At the same time, valuable nutrients are removed from the forest floor. The rivers will return to normal, and, with enough time, the forests will grow again, yet the fish populations may never be restored.

In northern California, the Forest Service is attempting to preserve habitat for the endangered northern spotted owl. Under the Pacific Northwest Forest Plan, the Shasta-Trinity National Forest in California was designated as habitat for the northern spotted owl and other species that depend upon late successional and old-growth forests. But root rot has turned this forest into what is now called the Valley of Death. In this once-magnificent forest, giant trees crash to the forest floor, crumbling under their own weight. Each lost tree thins the overstory, which reduces the closed canopy favored by the owls. As a result, the Forest Service is losing the wildlife habitat it is attempting to preserve. A single pair of owls remains nested in the vicinity, but in the future it is unlikely that other species requiring mature forest habitat will find a home in this reserve.

In an effort to maintain the old-growth trees and owl habitat in this forest, the Forest Service's Pacific Northwest Forest Plan banned thinning and salvage harvesting. But the result is higher mortality from disease and insects as well as greater risk of catastrophic loss due to fire. In the McCloud region of the Shasta-Trinity National Forest, root disease and bark beetles have reached epidemic proportions, resulting in tree mortality as high as 80 percent in heavily infested areas. Frustrated by the maze of regulations in the forest plan, forest managers predict that it will be at least several more years before any treatment to halt the infestation takes place. Meanwhile, the area of tree mortality continues to expand, destroying approximately three hundred additional acres each year. Plans for restoration must now include the high cost of removing the fuel buildup of dead trees, rather than the revenue that could have been generated earlier from a thinning or salvage operation to improve forest health.[7]

In northern Arizona, the area around Flagstaff was once known as Antelope Springs. Savanna-type forests provided an abundance of grasses and forage preferred by antelope. Today, few antelope are seen there. Dense tree growth and thick canopies have reduced forage and grasses. While the antelope have moved away, the threatened goshawk has moved in, making these forests its home. Yet the dense overgrown nature of the forests places this goshawk habitat at great risk of catastrophic fire.

Finally, elk are disappearing from the Clearwater National Forest in Idaho, once considered a paradise for wildlife. Much of the Clearwater basin burned in the great fires of 1910 that were the impetus for the fire suppression policies adopted by the Forest Service. Since then, the forest has been managed in the absence of fire, resulting in an even-aged stand of dense fir. Without the openings and meadows historically created by fire, the elk have nowhere to graze. The dense thicket of undergrowth blocks the sunlight and prevents the growth of essential forage. Over time, elk and other wildlife species have virtually disappeared from the forest ecosystem.[8]

Public concern has prompted federal managers to act. In the late 1990s, local citizens, the Forest Service, and the U.S. Fish and Wildlife Service came together to seek solutions and lure the elk back into the Clearwater. The group agreed on a wildlands fire plan to allow wildfires to burn for the benefit of the resources. The area covers 100,000 acres of desolate timberland in central Idaho. Even so, fires continue to be suppressed.

Land managers still perceive the risks of uncontrolled wildfire as too high. Even when the benefits of a fire would exceed the costs, managers do not want to assume that responsibility. "If you can't let a wildfire burn in central Idaho, you can't let it burn anywhere," says Greg Serveen, wildlife program coordinator for the Idaho Fish and Game Department.[9] Although the land is publicly owned, with no structures for miles around, fires are still snuffed out and the elk are still scarce.

PRIVATE MANAGEMENT

Private industrial land managers, in contrast, cannot afford to let their trees be devastated by insects, disease, or fire. Motivated by profits, these managers thin their forests and treat them to keep out disease and insects. Industrial forests, which make up about 10 percent of the nation's forestland, are managed to produce wood and paper products. They are generally maintained in young to middle-age stands, which are less susceptible to insects and disease. It is true that forests managed in this way may lack the species diversity associated with more complex forest structures. Increasingly, however, the value of recreation and conservation of diversified forest types is being realized and private managers are moving toward more multi-aged stands, which encourage more diversity of wildlife.

Boise Cascade owns a forest adjoining the insect-infested Willowa-Whitman National Forest in northeastern Oregon. But unlike Willowa-Whitman, Boise Cascade has had minimal loss from insect damage.[10] Managers have encouraged species such as ponderosa pine and Douglas fir and in many cases have maintained timber stands that are a close replica of the forests that stood in the Blue Mountains a hundred years ago. Selective harvesting creates a patchwork of openings that attract many plant and animal species. The clearings allow sunlight to reach the forest floor and encourage a variety of plants.

Commercial cuts can be designed to resemble the mosaic patterns typically found in historic forests.

Private timberlands are intermixed in the Shasta-Trinity National Forest. Like the national forest, the private land was originally logged at the turn of the century and has since grown into a forest providing late successional habitat similar to old-growth. The private forests, however, have been thinned, and salvage timber has been harvested. These forests provide habitat for the northern spotted owl while having a reduced risk of wildfire because of their low fuel loads. The landowners' primary objective is to grow and harvest quality forest products, but to do this they must also maintain forest health. Because of active management, their forests provide a variety of other forest values, such as wildlife habitat, clean water, and recreation.

Profits can provide a compelling incentive to improve habitat and attract new species demanded by a paying public. Two examples, International Paper and the White Mountain Apache tribe, illustrate how the search for revenues can lead to better stewardship.

International Paper Company

In Arkansas, Louisiana, and Texas, International Paper Company (IP) long provided public access to its 1.2 million acres of private timberland. Summer campouts, fall hunting trips, and year-round rambles in fragrant pine forests were a treasured part of life for thousands of outdoor enthusiasts. Because the Southeast does not have the vast public lands that are found in the West, residents long relied on the generosity of IP to provide them with free use of the land. Despite this heavy recreational use, the company managed its lands with one goal in mind: timber production, the main source of its revenue.

By the early 1980s, however, the steadily increasing demand for recreation and an innovative biologist by the name of Tom Bourland, convinced company executives to charge fees for recreation. Through the sale of daily use permits, seasonal family permits, and multiyear leases to hunting clubs, the company began generating significant revenues (Anderson and Leal 1997, 4–8). From zero in 1980, revenues grew to $2 million in 1986, representing 25 percent of the company's total profits in that region (Anderson and Leal 1997, 6). By 1999, the earnings from nontimber sources were $5 million.[11]

As the profits grew, so did the incentive to manage the forests for recreation as well as timber. To keep such revenues coming, the company had to improve wildlife habitat. So it began to take steps such as maintaining corridors of trees between logging areas to allow wildlife movement. In areas that previously would have been clear-cut, clumps of trees were left standing to provide greater age diversity and thus provide food for a greater variety of animals. The overall size of the timber cuts was reduced and the perimeters made irregular, creating more "edge," making the areas more attractive to more wildlife. Logging was restricted along streams in order to help maintain consistent water temperature and improve fish habitat. Long-term contracts with hunting clubs provided an incentive for the club members to act as stewards of the land they leased and to work cooperatively with IP managers.

These efforts paid big dividends to both wildlife and stockholders. Game surveys in 1996 showed that populations of whitetail deer increased fivefold and turkey tenfold, along with substantial increases in fox, quail, ducks, and nongame populations. The incentive for IP to change its land management came from the revenues generated by fee-based recreation programs and the growing interest in sustainable forest management.

IP completed certification on all of its U.S. forestland holdings according to standards set by the Sustainable Forestry Initiative program and to the International Organization for Standardization (ISO) 14001 environmental management system. Environmental management certification requires a third party to assess the sustainability of management performance and forest conditions.

More recently, in the fall of 2006 IP sold a large portion of its timberland holdings in the United States in a move to transform the company and focus more on processing than timber production. Much of the timberland was sold to a timberland investment management firm under terms that ensure continued forest certification.[12]

White Mountain Apache

Although an Indian tribe is not a private company, the opportunity for revenues for the tribe provided an incentive for Arizona's White Mountain Apache tribe to improve elk habitat on the reservation. Before 1977, the Arizona Game and Fish Department had managed hunting on the reservation. Like many state wildlife agencies, its goal was to maximize the number of hunter days, so it issued seven hundred annual elk permits for the reservation, at $150 each.

In 1977 the White Mountain Apache tribe took control of hunting on the reservation and made some drastic changes. In its first year of operation, the tribe issued just twelve permits, at a price of $750 each. The goal was to allow the elk on the reservation to grow to trophy size. Today, through careful management, the tribe has arguably the best elk herd in North America. Only thirty permits are issued each year for trophy bull elk, and they cost upward of $20,000 each. The waiting list for a permit is two to three years.[13]

To improve the quality of the herd, the tribe not only reduced hunting pressure but also hired biologists to assist with land management. Open meadows were protected, livestock grazing was reduced, and logging was restricted in the high country, riparian zones, and mountain meadows. But timber was still a top-revenue producer, earning $7 million a year in 1992 (Cornell and Kalt 1992, 224).

In 2002, the Rodeo-Chediski fire burned across nearly 300,000 acres of the White Mountain Apache Reservation, eliminating lower elevation pinyon-juniper forests and vast areas of ponderosa pine forest. Millions of dollars in timber value went up in smoke. After the fire, however, the tribe responded quickly, seeding over half of the burned landscape before summer's end and quickly removing much of the burned timber. With the good fortune of high precipitation the following winter, "outstanding" habitat is the result as new seedlings sprout on the burnt-over landscape.[14]

STATE STEWARDSHIP

State land managers face incentives that more closely resemble those affecting private owners than their federal counterparts. As discussed in the previous chapter, state land trusts are required to generate revenues to support schools and other public entities. They can sell timber and other commodities only if revenues received cover the costs of sale preparation and land restoration. In addition, the state managers must weigh the value of harvest or extraction in the present compared to the expected value in the future, or the expected value of forgoing the commodity removal and instead providing for land conservation. The requirement to obtain revenues affects stewardship, as the following examples indicate.

Forest Roads

State roads built to remove timber from the forests are usually temporary. Engineered at a low cost, they ensure environmental and personal safety during harvest, but then are removed to prevent future erosion. Building specifications are much lower than federal standards because of the planned short-term use. For example, in Montana a state timber road costs about $5,000 per mile and is built solely for the purpose of timber removal and reforestation. The fact that state managers must generate a positive return for public schools prevents overinvestment in roads, and many roads are routinely obliterated, eliminating the threat of environmental damage as well as the need for maintenance. Some are retained as foot trails for recreational use. In some states, such as Arizona, Montana, and New Mexico, a small fee is charged for recreation on state lands (see Fretwell 1998, 13–14).

In contrast, roads built to access federal timber sales are usually permanent, built to high specifications that can provide recreational access to the forest long after the timber has been cut and removed. In fact, there are 380,000 miles of Forest Service roads, a distance eight times longer than our interstate highway system (Fretwell 1999a, 26). And they are built to carry heavy traffic and remain in perpetuity. These high-quality roads are expensive projects; in 1997, the average cost for one mile of Forest Service road was $64,000 (FS 1998a, 163). Ninety-eight percent of the roads are used for recreation although they are paid for with congressional appropriations for the timber-harvesting program. Recreational users pay nothing for these roads—neither for their construction nor for their maintenance.

In the past, congressional appropriations for road building have created an incentive to build more and more roads in the national forests. The projects provided work for Forest Service engineers, planners, and other staff, expanding the size of the agency. Furthermore, forest managers would add roads for recreational use in order to meet their annual goals; the more roads, the higher their performance rating.

Forest Service roads provide millions of Americans easy access to the nation's forests. Driving through Montana's Gallatin National Forest in October is an awe-inspiring trip. The vibrant yellows and oranges of the aspens and cottonwoods mix with the deep greens of pine and spruce to create an arresting tapestry. Thousands of recreationists are drawn into the forest for a weekend drive or an end-of-season campout. Cars, trucks, RVs, ATVs, and mountain bikes crowd the road, sending plumes of dust into the air.

But the excessive number of roads running through the forests is beginning to take a toll on the environment. During the first half of the century, roads were built to much lower standards though still meant to be permanent. Many of these roads are now deteriorating, causing hillside erosion, water quality degradation, and other environmental problems. Though road construction and reconstruction has been brought to a near halt, the fact remains that not even 20 percent of forest roads are maintained to planned standards.[15] Federal forest managers have few funds to make repairs or, alternatively, to obliterate timber roads.

Viewsheds

State land managers have flexibility that federal managers do not, as this experience in Montana illustrates. In the 1980s a developer planned a new housing development on high rolling hills outside of Bozeman that would offer magnificent views of the surrounding mountains. At the same time, the state was making plans to harvest timber on Mount Ellis, which rises directly behind the new development. The mountain provided a stunning backdrop to the new Eagle Rock development, and the proposed cut did not sit well with new property owners or the developers, and they raised a ruckus with the state.

The state offered to stop the harvest if the homeowners agreed to pay for the timber as well as for what would normally grow again on the site during the next twenty years. The price for this "viewshed easement" came to $430,000. This may have been an accurate reflection of the value of two timber rotations, but it was more than the homeowners were willing to pay.

The state did not give up, however. The state came up with a less expensive alternative that saved the view and still earned a profit. The harvest was designed to mimic the natural mosaic of meadows caused by wind and fire, so almost as much timber was cut, but the harvest was barely discernible from a distance. This successful effort to satisfy local residents added only 1 or 2 percent to the overall logging costs, making the sale of 1.1 million board feet profitable for both the state school fund and the logging contractor (Fretwell 1999a, 26).

Solutions of this sort are not so easy to come by when dealing with federal agencies. Just over the ridge in the Gallatin National Forest, the Forest Service clear-cut the side of a mountain. The clear-cut became known as the "diaper line" because, when covered with snow from October to April, the two large, perfectly rectangular cuts strung below a straight logging road resembled diapers hung out to dry. The public outcry was deafening and continued for years. Local groups petitioned the Forest Service to harvest additional timber around the edges of the cut to soften the harsh lines and make the openings appear more natural. This was impossible, however, because the Forest Service had imposed a moratorium on timber harvesting to protect the watershed.[16]

Thirteen years passed before this Bozeman Creek sale was reharvested to feather the edges of the clear-cut. While working toward its timber volume goal, the Forest Service apparently did not anticipate the public backlash from the highly visible clear-cut. Caught in the political turmoil, the agency found that its own regulations rendered it powerless for more than a decade to modify the cut and quell the outcry.

FEDERAL INITIATIVES

As these examples show, federal stewardship is hampered by inappropriate incentives, excessive regulations, and litigation. Managers are forced to respond first to a political agenda rather than resource needs.

Although at the onset the picture appears grim, there is reason for optimism. In recent years, small but significant changes have altered the way federal land managers can care for the land. These new approaches include new fee programs and stewardship contracts.

Fees

Located deep in the red rock canyon country of southeastern Utah, Natural Bridges National Monument is the destination of nearly 150,000 visitors a year.[17] Meandering streams have cut through sandstone walls to form some of the world's largest natural bridges. Hiking the trails of this remarkable monument is the main attraction for tourists, who have also been the source of serious damage to the area's fragile ecosystem.

The delicate surface soils found in this arid region form a living crust that is particularly vulnerable to the compression stress of footprints or tires. To avoid mud holes and degraded portions of trail, visitors often walk outside the designated trails and as a result damage the crust, making it vulnerable to wind and water erosion. Affected areas are slow to recover, taking fifty years or longer. Despite deteriorating conditions in many areas of the monument, managers have received no money from Congress for trail improvements or repairs for the last thirteen years.

Historically, recreation fees collected on federal lands such as Natural Bridges were returned to the national treasury, except for a small percentage that was retained to fund the fee collection program.

The Fee Demonstration Program, authorized by Congress in 1996, and extended in 2004 by the Federal Lands Recreation Enhancement Act, has begun to change management incentives at Natural Bridges and throughout the federal domain. Participating sites are allowed to keep at least 60 percent of the fees earned at the site, with the remainder returned to the land agency to be used at nonparticipating units. In fiscal year 2001, Fee Demonstration Program revenues collected by the National Park Service totaled $126.2 million, the Forest Service collected $35.3 million, the Fish and Wildlife Service collected $3.7 million, and the Bureau of Land Management collected $7.6 million (USDI and USDA 2002, 5). Total recreation revenues have more than doubled since the onset of the program.

At Natural Bridges, the fees have allowed the managers to hire a trail supervisor and crew and to buy tools and materials to operate a sustainable trails program. The crew has reconstructed 5,000 feet of trails that were hazardous to visitors and damaging to the natural resource. They have also made repairs to another seven miles of trails. Plans call for more reconstruction of trails that are literally falling apart and repairs to eroded areas.

The new fees paid by recreational users have allowed managers to respond to the needs of the visitors and protect the natural resources in ways that were impossible when all funding for the monument was coming from congressional appropriations. The Federal Lands Recreation Enhancement Act of 2004 extended the Fee Demonstration Program until 2014 and may include any unit of the federal estate.

Contracts

The Lolo National Forest in northern Montana is suffering many of the same problems that have become common throughout the national forest system. Fire suppression since the 1930s has resulted in dense tree growth, while a history of logging has left a web of roads that fragment wildlife habitat and contribute to stream sedimentation.

Historically, the Clearwater area of the forest has been critical habitat for grizzly bears as a migration route between the Bob Marshall and Mission Mountain wilderness areas. The dense forest, however, has made travel for the grizzlies difficult. Bull trout, listed as threatened in 1998, also claim the area as one of their few remaining habitats. The forest keeps the shallow creeks cool during hot summer months, but sediment occasionally buries the trout's gravel spawning beds.

Forest managers were aware of serious problems on the Lolo. The mature forest was at grave risk of an infestation of mountain pine beetles and wildfire. Either occurrence would jeopardize the cover for bear migration and bull trout spawning. The Forest Service developed a treatment plan that called for the removal of some of the timber to improve forest health, the obliteration of some roads and the upgrading of others to reduce stream sedimentation, and the replacement of old pit toilets to improve water quality and visitor comfort.

A timber sale could raise money for the forest thinning, but no funds were available for the other treatment goals. District ranger Tim Love looked outside of the box to accomplish all the forest goals. Love designated the area for stewardship contracting, an adaptive management system with expanded contracting authorities. Stewardship contracts are another form of experimental management being tried by the Forest Service. A stewardship contract allows managers to use timber sale revenues as payment for other contracted services or to exchange goods for services. In the Clearwater area of the Lolo National Forest the contract was awarded to Pyramid Mountain Lumber, a small family operation eager to participate in the innovative stewardship project. The company agreed to do the work necessary to achieve the results prescribed by the forest management team and accept the timber that it cut as payment for its services.

In the end, about 2.5 million board feet will be harvested from 570 acres. The trees removed have been selected by Pyramid under a contract that they provide a predetermined end result in the forest, with monitoring built into the contract. Both the Swan Ecosystem Center and a citizen-based, multiparty monitoring team are helping to ensure accountability.

Thinning and clearing will create openings for forage, and prescribed burns will leave fire-killed trees for habitat enhancement. Nearly fifty miles of road will be obliterated to increase grizzly bear security and reduce sediment sources. Old-style pit toilets will be replaced with concrete vault toilets to improve water quality and sanitation. And harvested timber will be sent to the company's Seeley Lake, Montana, mill, providing jobs for local contractors, loggers, and truckers.

Pyramid, which owns no timberland, relies on developing good relationships with landowners to secure timber contracts. In this case, the company developed a strong working relationship with the district ranger and the other concerned parties. The company is harvesting timber in exchange for providing services—noxious weed treatment, culvert replacement, and road removal, for example.

Initially critical of the process, conservation leaders who have toured the site are impressed by the results. These include Bill Meadows, president of the Wilderness Society, Carl Pope, the Sierra Club's executive director, and Roger Schlickeisen, president of the Defenders of Wildlife, to name a few. The benefits of the project are many, but particularly noteworthy is the establishment of trusting relationships between the community, local and national interest groups, and the Forest Service.

The increased flexibility provided through stewardship contracts enhances the ability of forest managers to meet the changing objectives of the agency (as will be discussed in chapter 7). A transparent collaborative effort increases credibility, while accountability is provided through multiparty monitoring. The exchange of goods for services provides funds to carry out the activities. "Only imagination," says Love, can limit the possibilities of stewardship under the contract. The flexibility and new authorities have provided managers of the Lolo with a means to care for the land in a way that makes them proud.

CONCLUSION: MANAGEMENT INCENTIVES

Part of the message of this chapter is that Americans are not getting the stewardship they pay for. Although hundreds of millions of dollars are spent on our federal lands every year to ensure ecological health, productivity, and biodiversity, many landscapes exhibit almost none of these values. Instead, they are inhospitable to both wildlife and recreational visitors, and at risk of devastation from disease, insects, and catastrophic wildfire.

Yet other landscapes exhibit healthy, vigorous ecosystems. Private landowners who grow trees for commercial harvest have a long-term commitment to the value of the timber and a strong incentive to manage for a productive forest. Ranchers must ensure the long-term viability of rangelands to remain profitable. In recent years, the growing market in outdoor recreation has created additional incentives for private owners to manage their lands for wildlife, recreational opportunities, and other environmental amenities. Similarly, the managers of state trust lands have shown that with less political interference and clear mandates to generate revenues for public schools, public lands can be managed to benefit both state residents and the health of the land.

Contrary to the assumptions of many environmentalists, logging and grazing have a role to play in securing the financial and ecological health of the land. Another part of the message of this chapter is that federal managers are looking for ways to restore our public lands to health and productivity. They are trying experiments that seem to work. The challenge is to apply them on a larger scale.

NOTES

1. Telephone communication with John Hoffman, Vice President of Government Affairs, California Forestry Association, Sacramento, California, December 5, 1998.

2. National Parks Conservation Association, "Across the Nation," available at http://www.npca.org/across_the_nation/AmericansforNationalParks/about/default.asp.

3. Wildlife Service Survey, available at http://www.ucsusa.org/scientific_integrity/interference/us-fish-wildlife-service-survey.html. Cited May 18, 2006.

4. As defined in the Federal Land Policy and Management Act of 1976 (43 U.S.C.A. Sec. 1701).

5. As defined by the Organic Act of 1916 (16 U.S.C.A. Sec. 1).

6. Most states are beginning to provide for conservation leases to. allow those lands more highly valued as open space to remain so.

7. Written communication from Nancy Ingalsbee, Klamath Alliance for Resources and Environment, Yreka, California, January 12, 1999.

8. Telephone communication with Greg Serveen, Environmental Staff Biologist, Idaho Fish and Game, Lewiston, Idaho, September 21, 1998.

9. Ibid., May 12, 2003.

10. Data in this section were provided through written and phone communication with Cassandra Botts, Communications Manager, Boise Cascade, Joseph, Oregon, September 1, 1998, and February 1999.

11. Telephone communication with Tom Bourland, wildlife biologist, Crawford and Bourland, Inc., Shreveport, Louisiana, May 26, 1999. Bourland was previously wildlife manager of IP's mid-south region.

12. International Paper Investor Information News Release, available at http://investor.internationalpaper.com/phoenix.zhtml?c=73062&p=irol-newsArticle&ID=9 26693&highlight=.

13. Telephone communication with Jesse Palmer, Wildlife Biologist, White Mountain Apache Wildlife and Outdoor Recreation Division, May 1, 2003.

14. Telephone communication with Jesse Palmer, Wildlife Biologist, White Mountain Apache Wildlife and Outdoor Recreation Division, May 1, 2003.

15. USDA Forest Service, Road Management Website, available at http://www.fe.fed.us/eng/road_mgt/overview.shtml.

16. Interview of Kimberly Schlenker, Staff Assistant, Recreation Wilderness Landscape Management, Gallatin National Forest, Bozeman, Montana, October 7, 1998.

17. Written communication with Keith Stegall, SEUG Trails Coordinator, Canyon Lands National Park, Moab, Utah, December 18, 1998.

Chapter Four

Is No Use Good Use?

More and more federal land is being removed from multiple-use management and set aside for the preservation of landscapes, natural ecosystems, and biodiversity. This change from past practice carries with it enormous implications for the land and the public, who owns it.

DESIGNATIONS

To understand the potential costs of the change to "no use," we should first recognize how much federal land has been put into categories that drastically restrict its use. This has occurred through congressional designations, administrative designations, and executive designations.

Congressional

Through the legislative process, Congress has restricted multiple use on more than 20 percent of Forest Service lands. These lands have been designated as national wilderness areas, recreation areas, scenic areas, game refuges and wildlife reserves, wild and scenic rivers, and monuments.

The growth in wilderness acres alone has been dramatic. Wilderness is defined by legislation to mean areas that are undisturbed and natural, pristine and "untrammeled by man." Since the Wilderness Act of 1964, which set aside 9 million acres of Forest Service land as wilderness, another 26 million acres of national forest has been assigned wilderness status. Far greater has been the addition of wilderness to the national park system, with 44 million acres. Even the Fish and Wildlife Service (FWS) and Bureau of Land Management can now boast 21 and 7 million acres of wilderness under their control, respectively.

Acreage under control of the National Park Service (NPS), lands managed for FWS refuges, and use restrictions on Bureau of Land Management lands have also increased. Since 1964, the amount of land congressionally designated in a restricted use category has quadrupled.

Administrative

Restrictions designated by the land management agencies are growing even faster. The Forest Service has more than thirty classifications that restrict lands from multiple use. Research natural areas are regions protected to maintain natural conditions for research and monitoring; areas of critical environmental concern are those designated to protect fish and wildlife or cultural and scenic values; special interest areas are locations protected for some unique characteristic such as an area with botanical or geological significance. Other classifications include natural areas, semiprimitive and primitive areas, restricted roadless areas, nonmotorized areas, and special management areas, to name a few.[1]

In addition, the federal agencies have put together several special plans that cover vast western territories. The Grizzly Bear Recovery Plan covers 23 million acres in the northern Rockies, limiting activities to protect bears and their habitat. The Northwest Forest Plan protects old-growth habitat on 24 million acres in the Pacific Northwest, prohibiting harvest on 19 million acres. The Sierra Nevada Framework outlines restrictive management on 11 million acres, protecting more than 4 million acres of old forest and using tree diameter to limit harvest elsewhere.

Executive

Past U.S. presidents have used executive designations to set aside lands.[2] President Bill Clinton proclaimed national monuments on 6 million acres, more than double the amount that President Theodore Roosevelt classified under the Antiquities Act of 1906 and second only to President Jimmy Carter, who set aside 58 million acres in Alaska.

Under the Clinton administration's directive, the Forest Service also proposed a protection plan for inventoried roadless areas not designated as wilderness, which prohibits road construction and restricts logging on 58.5 million acres of national forests. This could have effectively remove 37 percent of the remaining nonwilderness areas on national forests from multiple use. The Bush administration modified this designation by opening the final decisions to input from state governors. Federal lands designated for restricted use now total approximately 337 million acres (see table 4.1).

Table 4.1. Federal Land Designated Use Acreage

	Million Acres	
	1964	*2000*
Forest Service		
Designated wilderness area	9	35
Other designated use areas	7	68
Total designated areas (%)	16 (9%)	103 (54%)
All Federal Land Management Agencies		
Designated wilderness area	9	105
Other designated use areas	57	232
Total designated areas (%)	66 (11%)	337 (55%)

Private Lands

Private lands have also come under federal control in the name of environmental protection. The Wetlands Reserve Program restricts about 1.5 million acres of private land to wetland use, preventing landowners from developing their land if the acreage has been declared wetlands. It is federal policy to avoid a "net loss" of wetlands.[3] The Conservation Reserve Program pays farmers to keep 34 million acres of private farmland out of productive use.[4] More than 39 million acres of private land are controlled by Habitat Conservation Plans[5] and more than 1 million acres are under Safe Harbor Agreements.[6] These two programs require landowners to set aside portions of their land for wildlife protected under the Endangered Species Act, but free them from use restrictions on their remaining land.

In sum, more than 500 million acres of land are set aside under stringent land-use restrictions by federal mandate. This is an area three times the size of Texas, or 20 percent of the entire nation. The fiscal and ecological implications of these set-asides are enormous.

THE HIGH COSTS OF HANDS-OFF MANAGEMENT

These set-asides, together with the decline in logging and grazing, have forced the Forest Service and other federal land management agencies to revert to a more custodial management style typical of earlier times. But this shift from active to passive management comes at great cost. Some of these costs are financial. Local communities suffer from lost jobs and business activity as sawmills close down, and they face increased risk of wildfire. The nation's taxpayers lose revenues from their natural assets. But there are other costs, including shrinking recreational access and, especially, the increasing difficulty of providing good land stewardship. This chapter will examine the effects of "no use."

Higher Costs, Fewer Commodities

Eliminating commodity production has reduced the revenues available for management. Since the late 1980s, timber output from federal lands has declined more than 80 percent, a reduction of more than 10 billion board feet (FS 2000b, 224). While national forests contain 37 percent of the nation's softwood timber supply, they are producing only 5 percent of our consumption.

Timber harvests on federal lands in Oregon and Washington have fallen from more than 6 billion board feet per year in the late 1980s to around 600 million board feet in 2006. This is in one of the most productive timber-growing regions in the world. One acre of forest in the Pacific Northwest can provide as much timber as four or more acres elsewhere.[7] To restrict harvest on 20 million acres here may mean that as many as 80 million acres will be harvested somewhere else.

Timber receipts have declined from an inflation-adjusted $1.8 billion to around $500 million (FS 1999, table 52). But the costs of the timber program show no reciprocal decline. The cost of offering 1,000 board feet of timber for sale has risen from $53 to $182 (O'Toole 1998, 2000). While the overall agency budget has continued to hover around $3.5 billion annually since 1988, timber output and revenues have fallen (OMB 1999) (see chapter 2).

Likewise, proposals to eliminate grazing rarely consider the cost of management without the cattle. Managing the federal grazing lands costs $120 million annually, with a return close to $20 million. Even if livestock were to be removed, management of the land without cattle would not be free. In fact, while cattle numbers on the federal estate have decreased, range expenditures have risen (see chapter 2).

Not widely known is the fact that about half of all federal timber receipts are used for forest restoration. These activities include replanting, improving remaining stands, habitat enhancement, stream restoration, trail and road maintenance, and facility construction; the list goes on (GAO 1998c, 16–19).[8] As noted in chapter 2, a portion of sales receipts are deposited into the Knutson-Vandenberg (K-V) Fund and made available to field managers for ecological management. This fund was established in 1930 to protect and improve all resource values on timber sale areas. Often these are the only monies available to managers for stewardship activities, yet K-V funds have dropped by 50 percent since 1995.[9]

Lack of funds has become a major problem on many national forests. Santa Fe National Forest Supervisor Leonard Atencio attributes his lack of stewardship funds to the steep drop in commercial logging revenues. Though he should be thinning about 25,000 acres annually, he has the staff and money to thin just 2,000 acres (*Missoulian*, October 15, 2000). Without the K-V funds, restoration objectives will either be sacrificed or achieved in a more costly manner through the appropriation of tax dollars.

Even if timber revenues had continued to come in, however, tying stewardship funds to harvests is not a formula for responsible forest management. This long-standing arrangement prevents managers from being able to limit harvest yet conduct restoration projects. Without this authority and flexibility, they cannot manage their forests in a professional manner.

As regulations continue to increase, more resources are being concentrated in the Forest Service's Washington office while staff and funding for field offices are being reduced. Since 1991, the budget at the Washington headquarters has increased 118 percent more than inflation. In this same period, six of nine forest regions have seen their budgets decrease anywhere from 10 to 39 percent.[10] The ecological impacts of these declines can be significant.

- In 2000, Montana's Gallatin National Forest lost a thirteen-member trails crew due to reduced staff funding for the region.[11]
- In Washington State's Mount Baker-Snoqualmie National Forest, a trails crew that once numbered sixty dropped to twenty when the budget declined from $3.8 million in 1994 to $3 million in 2000 (Forsgren 2000, 1).
- President Clinton's roadless initiative cost $7.6 million for planning alone in 2000.[12] Furthermore, the new rule made years of costly study and forest planning at the local level irrelevant.

LITIGATION AND APPEALS

In addition to facing cutbacks in improvement projects due to lack of revenues, the Forest Service is virtually paralyzed by litigation and appeals. In the past, there was justification for appeals, because the Forest Service planning process, excessively motivated by the desire to log, was probably cutting down trees where they should not have been cut. Today the problem is largely reversed.

To reduce the risk of catastrophic fire, thinning is essential in many areas that are fire-prone. In 2000, 48 percent of all timber sales were designed for stewardship purposes. Yet many of these sales were postponed or precluded by litigation and appeals (FS 2000–2002, 6–36), primarily by environmental groups that think they are helping the forest.

In Santa Fe, New Mexico, the Forest Guardians, a nationally known advocacy group, has dedicated itself to ending all commercial logging on federal lands. One mission of the group is to "prevent these abuses [timber sales, grazing and mining permits, and oil and gas leasing] through strategic appeals and litigation (Forest Guardians 2000)." And yet in 2000, fires burned out of control in nearby Los Alamos, incinerating many of the forests this group hoped to preserve through zero-cut policies. In the aftermath, the group's executive director, Rex Wahl, sees the situation differently: "Judicious cutting of small trees is what's needed" (Grigg 2000) to prevent future catastrophe.

But that temporary change of heart did not lead the organization to reduce its effort to stop logging, even when the disastrous consequences are evident to others. About 1,500 acres of forest burn each year near Flagstaff, threatening community health, the economy, and the ecological integrity of the forest. To deal with this problem, several groups, including the Forest Service, the Grand Canyon Trust, and Northern Arizona University, as well as numerous local, state, and county officials, came together to form the Greater Flagstaff Forests Partnership (formerly the Grand Canyon Forests Partnership). This collaborative partnership set out to analyze 10,000 acres annually and come up with a plan that would thin the forests surrounding Flagstaff and reduce the risk of catastrophic fire that would threaten the community. Harvest goals were set based on community desires and approach conditions similar to those before European settlement. Appropriate treatment would reduce the risk of catastrophic fire and serve as a demonstration project for other communities.

Implemented in 1998 and exempt from public input and appeals, the first project compared different restoration prescriptions removing different amounts of timber from sections of a 300-acre plot. Based on the information gathered in the first project, the second project was designed to treat 9,000 acres and to be the first in a series of landscape-scale ecosystem restorations.

Appeals and lawsuits have been filed against the completed environmental assessment. Appellants include the Forest Guardians, the National Forest Protection Alliance, and the Forest Conservation Council. Meanwhile, catastrophic fires near Flagstaff not only burn up trees but also damage wildlife. These fires do more damage every year to habitat for the endangered goshawk and the Mexican spotted owl than any other forest activity.[13] Tunnel vision by zero-cut environmental groups often prevents or slows progress on even well-researched experimental programs that have broad community support. The pilot project to restore national forest land surrounding Flagstaff, Arizona, is just one example.

In many cases, the public input process required in national forest management is dominated by narrow interests such as the Forest Guardians and other like-minded groups. As a result, rational forest planning and management by professionals is nearly impossible. Projects involving fuel reduction that were also open to appeal were contested 59 percent of the time for a total of about 450 appeals during fiscal years 2001 and 2002 (GAO 2002a, 27).[14] Although the Forest Service ultimately affirms the majority of the projects, appeals are a method by which special interests can dispute agency decisions at relatively low cost to them.

Environmental objectives suffer when managers are forced to abandon or postpone timber harvest goals because of a costly and lengthy planning process, appeals, and litigation. This has been revealed time and again:

- Following the fires of 2000 on the Bitterroot National Forest, the planning process delayed restoration efforts. Fire had swept across 307,000 acres in western Montana killing trees that could produce more than 1 billion board feet of timber. An already large beetle population, the result of several drought years and winter blowdowns, posed an imminent threat to the weakened trees. The Forest Service, determined to restore the landscape and prevent a beetle outbreak, set out to harvest 176 million board feet of timber. To ensure sufficient documentation and avoid delay the Forest Service assigned the equivalent of fifty-seven work years to planning the project, spending an estimated $1 million for analysis and document preparation (FS 2002, C-2). Nonetheless, litigation and appeal held up the process. Recovery action required a court-ordered mediation. A year and one-half after the fires, the agency negotiated a harvest of 60 million board feet of timber. Yet by spring 2003 only 36 million board feet had been sold, and only half of that had been removed from the forest.[15] As a result, beetle infestation has killed more trees than the wildfire.[16]
- In the fall of 2000, the Flathead National Forest in Montana withdrew one of its largest timber sales. The project would have thinned a dense, 3,000-acre ponderosa pine forest in order to restore the open-canopy typical of its historical structure. The sale was withdrawn when two environmental groups filed a lawsuit to require a supplemental environmental impact statement.
- In the Blue Mountains of Oregon, harvest on the Wallowa-Whitman National Forest declined from nearly 300 million board feet a year in 1987 to less than 50 million in 1997. At the same time, loss to bug depredation is growing. Although insects are a natural part of the forest, years of fire

suppression and other past management practices have left the forest extremely dense and thus highly susceptible to insect infestation and disease in epidemic proportions (Fretwell 1999a).

- Pine beetle infestations in the southwest have spread repeatedly from federal to neighboring private lands. The environmental analysis process was too time-consuming to allow removal of infested trees before their spread (FS 2002, 28).
- In 2000, the Forest Service withdrew fifty-six timber sales on dozens of national forests across the South. Though many of these sales were intended to create habitat and restore ecosystems for endangered, threatened, and sensitive species, the Sierra Club and other environmental groups challenged them. A habitat restoration project on the Ouachita National Forest in Arkansas for the endangered red-cockaded woodpecker was just one of the resulting abandoned sales (McCabe 2001, 4).[17]
- In 1995, a California winter storm downed nearly 35,000 acres of trees on the Six Rivers National Forest. Managers proposed a salvage and restorative treatment to reduce the fuel load and wildfire risk. The next three years were spent in planning and analysis and responding to appeals. Only 1,600 acres were successfully treated. Nature took control during the fall of 1999, burning all untreated acreage plus an additional 90,000 acres. Managers have returned to ground zero in the process to restore the burned-over landscape (FS 2002, 7).

Many Forest Service officials, frustrated by the delays, fear that the problem will worsen. They believe that more set-asides, like the roadless initiative proposed under the Clinton administration, will hamper their ability to restore and maintain ecological sustainability (GAO 2000b, 28). Current forest plans already restrict road construction on 20.5 million acres of the inventoried roadless areas identified in 1979 and restricted in use under the Clinton administration roadless rule.

The remaining inventoried roadless areas, covering nearly 40 million acres, are now subject to new determination. Decisions will be based on Forest Service directives considering input from state governors. The local input will help provide perspective from those most affected by the forest management decisions. The Roadless Area Conservation National Advisory Committee has been formed to advise the Secretary of Agriculture on management and conservation of roadless areas and petitions submitted by states.

Many environmental groups applauded the roadless rule but the long-term consequences of a one-size-fits-all set-aside would have been devastating, and the impact of the rule as currently modified is uncertain. In Idaho, the Payette National Forest could be forced to abandon plans to restore an overly dense ponderosa pine forest. In California, the Shasta-Trinity National Forest might be unable to reduce hazardous fuels in a key watershed containing critical habitat for the threatened northern spotted owl. In Colorado, the Routt National Forest might have to forgo thinning of roadless areas immediately adjacent to private dwellings, leaving the forest highly susceptible to catastrophic wildfire (GAO 2000b, 25–26). Under the Bush administration, governors may petition for their desired land use in existing roadless areas, but mistrust of the Forest Service has many environmental groups concerned about any new activity that may be allowed in the inventoried roadless areas.

The last half-century has added regulations and restrictions that are increasing costs and confrontations between the agency and the public. The late Senator Hubert Humphrey sponsored the National Forest Management Act in 1976 for the very purpose of involving the public in Forest Service planning, with the goal of reducing conflict. Humphrey said the act would mean that "forest managers could practice forestry in the forest and not in the courts" (quoted in Fedkiw 1996, 193). Ironically, increased public participation has only intensified the debate over federal land use. The number of appeals rose from more than 1,000 per year at the end of the 1980s to more than 2,600 by 1993 (Fedkiw 1996, 193, 212).

While those living closest to the forest bear the greatest burden of management delays, agency actions that are the subject of protests and appeals can appear insignificant in the overall realm of federal forest health issues. The acreage affected by appeals on fuel reduction projects is relatively small; about 6 percent of all federal forestlands are found to be in poor health as a result of fire suppression. But the cost to the Forest Service is substantial. It has been estimated that 40 percent of work at the national forest level is for planning and assessment at a cost of more than $250 million annually (FS 2002, 5).

Because the Forest Service is trying to appease public groups and avoid litigation, costs to prepare timber sales on national forests have increased by as much as 25 to 33 percent from the late 1980s to the early 1990s. The Wallowa-Whitman National Forest is a typical example. By 1992, the aggregate timber management costs on the Wallowa-Whitman were $125 per thousand board feet. The comparable cost to produce 1,000 board feet of lumber for industrial producers was $53, for the Bureau of Indian Affairs $25, and for the Idaho Department of Lands just $9 (McKetta and Weiner 1994, 11).

Sale preparation costs are increasing faster than agency expectations (FS 2000b, 154). The Forest Service's real paralysis, says Jan Lerum, Forest Service Region 10 Ecosystem Planner, is the extended analysis required to avoid the further delays of an appeal. Even so, many decisions are still appealed and litigated at additional cost and delay. There is great pressure on managers to choose harvest and restoration areas that will provoke the least resistance. After working for more than thirty years in the Department of Agriculture, John Fedkiw believes that "appeals and court actions became costly major obstacles to achieving the congressionally established and funded timber targets" (1996, 140).

Indeed, achieving timber harvest goals is no longer a priority for the Forest Service. Expectations that harvest goals will not be met are common as managers run into more obstacles between the planning and harvesting stages. Large wildfires and the costs associated with firefighting provide additional reasons to expect delays in reaching timber goals.

A case in point is Montana's Bitterroot National Forest, where wildfire burned 335,000 acres in 2000. Before the burns, Cathy Stewart, the former forest manager of the Bitterroot, wanted to treat a roadless area of the forest containing high biomass accumulation. Selective harvest and brush removal would have provided openings for wildlife, encouraged forage, and reduced the dense structure of the forest. The goal was to restore the forest's natural resilience. Despite the sound science behind this proposal and others like it, public input and controls imposed from Washington, D.C., make this type of active management in remote areas a near impossibility. It is also more expensive to negotiate sales in remote regions. Instead of basing her decision on the scientific evidence, Stewart made a pragmatic decision based on politics.[18] She dedicated agency resources to treating more easily accessible acres at a lower cost in order to meet timber plan goals.

The labyrinthine requirements of forest planning today have made it impossible for the Forest Service to carry out its plan for saving the northern spotted owl. A battle to preserve habitat for the northern spotted owl, a listed threatened species, prompted years of litigation and delayed timber harvests in the forests of the Pacific Northwest during the 1980s. To "end the gridlock within the federal government," 24 million acres of federal land were reserved under a newly created Northwest Forest Plan (FS 1994, 3). Most of that land, 19 million acres, was preserved for old-growth habitat, while timber harvest was allowed on the remaining 5 million acres.

Yet even in the areas where logging is permitted, timber removal has been minimal. It was anticipated that 1.1 billion board feet of timber would be harvested every year from within the forest plan boundaries, but in 2003, less than half that amount was offered for sale.[19] During the 1980s, typically more than 4 billion board feet of lumber had been removed annually from that area.

One cause for the harvest delay was the plan's requirement that field surveys and inventories be conducted for the presence of more than four hundred species of plants and animals before any action could be taken (FS 1994). Yet adequate scientific survey procedures to detect some of these species were not available then and are still not available today. The 2005 National Forest System Planning Rule reduced the effects of the survey and manage requirements to maintain wildlife viability. Regardless, and despite a good-faith effort to satisfy concerned special interest groups, costly appeals continue to prohibit and delay timber sales.

The concept of preserving habitat in an effort to prevent changes appears to be fundamentally flawed. Nature is dynamic. With or without human influence, the natural environment will change. "There is no essential nature out there waiting to be saved," says Nancy Langston (1995, 300), ecologist and professor of environmental studies at the University of Wisconsin, who reflects the current views of the ecology profession. The "essential" nature is constant change.

Preservation of northern spotted owl habitat in the Pacific Northwest is a case in point. Even though the old-growth habitat has been protected and, in fact, expanded, owl numbers continue to dwindle (Thomas et al. 2006, 284).

Preservation in other regions under the plan have seen declines in old-growth stands. In the Shasta-Trinity National Forest, active management was prohibited in old-growth and late seral reserves under the Northwest Forest Plan. Because the forest is wracked with disease and insects, weakened trees fall to the forest floor. Each lost tree thins the overstory, which reduces the closed canopy. This in turn eliminates habitat for those species that require a mature forest — not a dead and dying forest. Tree mortality is expanding at a rate of more than three hundred acres per year, but managers are unable to respond because of the forest's reserve status (Fretwell 1999a, 12). Meanwhile, old-growth species such as the northern spotted owl must look elsewhere for habitat.

RECREATION FACING NEW LIMITS

Even recreationists are feeling the effects of more restrictive land management policies. The national forests are the most widely used federal lands for recreation, and driving for pleasure is the number-one use of those lands (FS 1998b). Nearly every visitor to the national forests uses the extensive road system, and 99 percent of road use is by people using the forest for recreation such as scenic drives, camping, and picnicking (FS 2000b, 3–126).

As the population in western states grows, so too does the demand for recreation on the national forests. Yet, designations such as wilderness or wild and scenic limit the type of recreation that is possible. The Forest Service is also allocating more funds for road obliteration. Both of these policies limit public access and, as a consequence, more and more people will be recreating on less and less land. Concentrated land use increases degradation and diminishes the quality of the recreational experience.

The use of snowmobiles, ATVs, and other motorized vehicles has been under scrutiny on federal lands. As the popularity of off-road vehicle use rises, there is legitimate concern about the affects of unmanaged use. In the fall of 2005, the Forest Service announced a new travel management policy authorizing managers of the individual units of national forests and grasslands to identify and designate areas of use. Many of the proposed travel plans limit access to off-road vehicles.

The decentralization of this plan, however, should allow for a more localized examination of the costs and benefits of allowing for off-road use. Historically, such management decisions have been based more on the wishes of national political groups. The changing limits on snowmobile use in Yellowstone are a case in point. Yellowstone National Park has made the National Parks Conservation Association's annual list of America's ten most endangered national parks at least four years in a row, with continued snowmobile use cited as one of the park's greatest threats. A 1997 lawsuit forced the National Park Service to complete an environmental impact statement to determine winter use in Yellowstone and Grand Teton national parks and the John D. Rockefeller Jr. Memorial Parkway. Under the Clinton administration it was decided that snowmobiles would be phased out of the park over a period of several years. Once again, political influence held sway. When George W. Bush took office, policy changed to allow snowmobile use to continue at reduced levels, though with the provision that cleaner engines are used and tours guided.

TAKING HUMANS OUT OF THE ENVIRONMENT

Returning to passive management has ecological consequences that are just beginning to be felt. Although some environmental groups ignore the evidence, experts on forest health from many backgrounds agree that the national forests cannot "heal themselves"—at least not within a relevant human time frame. Fire ecologist Steve Arno insists that the forests need intensive human intervention—and even then restoration will take decades. "With management—thinning, harvesting, and a carefully controlled burning program designed to encourage growth of native plant and tree species—we can slowly reduce the risk of severe wildfires and disease, creating a more natural range of conditions, which is the first step in ecosystem restoration" (Peterson 2000, 14).

Many people believe that if America's forests are to be protected and re-stored, they should be left alone. Given several hundred years and nature's resilience, such a plan probably would return some form of a natural forest. But this type of hands-off management has consequences, as Chadwick Oliver, the Pinchot Professor of Forestry and Environmental Studies at Yale University, explains: "In a few hundred years, a more natural range of forest species would probably re-emerge, but there would be great suffering in the meantime. In many places, the air we breathe and the water we drink would be polluted; exotic plants and animals would invade our forests; lives would be lost and millions of acres of native habitat would be destroyed" (Peterson 2000, 15). A former chief of the Forest Service and wildlife biologist Jack Ward Thomas says, "Biologically speaking, eliminating harvesting, while continuing to control wildfires, would have significant adverse effects on bird and mammal species that thrive on early succession forest conditions" (Peterson 2000, 14).

Leaving our national forests untended is not the equivalent of keeping them wild. Humans have influenced forest systems through the use of fire for thousands of years. As we have seen, fire suppression and other past management practices have significantly altered the composition. Whether a forest is "natural" is in the eyes of the beholder. Following the last ice age, human influence on the forests of North America has occurred without interruption. For thousands of years native peoples used fire to clear the landscape for homes, agriculture, or to increase forage growth for wildlife habitat. Years later European settlement further altered the forested landscapes. Considering the many incarnations of forest over the last 12,000 years, it is worth asking which are more natural or which should be the benchmark for the forest restoration projects of today.

Today, these forests are more susceptible to wildfire, insect infestation, and disease.[20] Wildfires exceeding 8 million acres every year between 2004 and 2007, which were preceded by other years (1988, 1994, 1996, 1999, and 2000) of devastating wildfire, are strong evidence that the health of our federally managed lands has been compromised. Federal lands made up 62 percent of the burned lands in 2000, even though 80 percent of forests in the nation are privately owned (National Interagency Fire Center 2000).

According to the Forest Service, about 190 million acres remain at high risk of wildfire, though that number could be anywhere from 90 to 200 million acres (GAO 2003c, 14). Assistant Director of Planning for the Forest Service Douglas MacCleery says, "The twin problems of fuel build-ups and declining forest health, and their effect on ecosystem diversity and sustainability, are likely to be the single most significant environmental challenges facing federal forest managers over the next two decades" (1999, 4).

Shifting to custodial management now—as the Forest Service is doing—will only worsen the situation. Timber harvesting and livestock grazing
are not inherently bad; rather, it is poor management that is responsible for
damaging the ecological integrity of many forests and grasslands.

In the West, ponderosa pine forests that historically carried seventy trees
per acre now have as many as seven hundred trees per acre (*Missoulian*,
October 15, 2000). Competing for sunlight, nutrients, and moisture, the trees
are smaller and denser, making them more susceptible to insects, disease, and
wildfire. In the past, random wildfires created small openings among the trees
allowing plants to grow that were forage for wildlife. Today, the dense closed
canopies of these forests provide habitat for completely different species.

In the Midwest, forests of upland oaks benefited from occasional fire
disturbance that reduced competition (Olson 1996). These open forest types
have become closed stands, a process that alters the composition of the forest
and reduces the diversity of species.

In the South and East, where many national forests are second- or third-
growth stands, closed canopies are forming from lack of disturbance. Controversy over logging has so restricted harvests that once-common early
successional habitat is declining and the species dependent upon it are now
imperiled. For example, in the Cherokee National Forest in Tennessee populations of the golden-winged warbler could have been enhanced in the forest
if some harvest had been allowed. Instead, birds and other species dependent
upon early successional forests have to find homes elsewhere, because their
native forests are growing too old (McCabe 1999, 1–2).[21]

Even at high elevations where the effects of fire exclusion are less profound, some forests have undergone substantial ecological changes. Aspen
communities have declined, meadows and openings have diminished in size
or disappeared, and existing forest stands have overstory trees that are older
on the average than historical trends. Some lodgepole pine forests that evolved
with less frequent but more intense wildfires are growing into more unified
stands with little diversity. "The ecological diversity and 'patchy-ness' of the
forest landscape has been reduced," according to MacCleery (1999, 28).

Without fire disturbance or timber harvest, all these forests are moving
toward even-aged, mid-succession forests that are less diverse than either
young or old forest stands. Few species find their sole habitat in mid-succession stands (Peterson 2000, 14).

The city of Denver has already suffered the consequences of hands-off
forest management: Years of fire suppression in the forest surrounding the
city's main reservoir allowed small, thin-barked trees to proliferate. Without
active management of the site, the fuels accumulated and in conjunction with
drought wildfire eventually destroyed the city's main watershed. Twelve

thousand acres were burned in the Buffalo Creek fire of 1996. The rains that followed sent a twenty-foot wall of water into the reservoir, leaving a seventeen-foot sediment bank against the dam and taking two lives. In the five years following the fire, there were thirteen floods so severe that they were classified as hundred-year flood events. Denver has spent more than $3 million to restore its watershed and expects to spend at least $8 million more (Fretwell 2001, 15).

Without some form of human intervention, wildfires will continue to devastate forests that have been made more vulnerable to such catastrophic events through years of human management. And the aftermath of these fires can be as bad as the fires themselves and longer lasting. Bare, burned soils erode in seasonal rains. Sediments clog streams and muddy reservoirs, destroying fish populations and damaging drinking water for large populations.

DENSE FORESTS REDUCE WATER FLOW

One of the original reasons for the establishment of national forests under the 1897 Organic Act was to secure "favorable conditions of water flows." National forests are the single largest source of water in the United States (FS 2000e, 2). The streams and rivers that flow through our national forests provide municipal water for cities and towns throughout the nation. The extremely dense forests that are commonplace today consume far more water than the sparser forests of the past. The result is less water flowing off the forests into streams to meet the growing demand for water.

National forests are about 30 percent denser today than in 1952 and provide less water for downstream tributaries and streams (Wagner 1998, 6). Average water flow on the Platte River has declined 15 percent under Forest Service management.[22] This decline has been harmful to numerous species dependent on the Central Platte River in Nebraska. As a result, the Fish and Wildlife Service has listed the whooping crane, least tern, piping plover, pallid sturgeon, and others as endangered.

The river's flow could be restored through increased harvest in the watershed. The managers of the Medicine Bow, Arapaho, Roosevelt, and Routt national forests all have a voice in managing the Platte River watershed. The forest plans all indicate that increased water flow to the Platte River system can be provided without degrading water quality. Watershed research demonstrates that timber harvesting and vegetation removal can increase water yield (Bosch and Hewlett 1982). Without increasing stream sedimentation, timber harvesting can increase flows by as much as 50 percent (Troendle, Wilcox, and Bevenger 1998, 15).

The additional needed water could be supplied if the Forest Service met its timber targets in the region.[23] Instead, national forest timber sales have been well below those called for in forest plans. The national forests in the Platte River headwaters are being managed in a way that will continue to increase forest density and decrease water yield. These reduced stream flows affect recreation and agriculture as well as wildlife.

Timber management has been used successfully to augment water supplies in other areas. The Boston metropolitan area draws significant supplies of water from the Quabbin Reservoir, which was built in the 1930s. By 1970, there were plans to expand the water system by diverting water from the Connecticut River at a cost in excess of $80 million. Seeking a more cost-effective alternative, Quabbin forest managers proposed increasing the available water by increasing the forest harvest. By clearing stands of red pine to create meadows, more water flowed into the reservoir. This forest treatment, combined with conservation measures that reduced consumption by increasing price, enabled the existing reservoir to meet growing water demands.[24] The managers continue to maintain a healthy and diverse forest cover including critical habitat for more than thirty threatened or endangered species. This was the first public forest in the United States to be certified by the Forest Stewardship Council as practicing sustainable management.

Regardless of the evidence linking forest density to water yield, managers are not rewarded for increased water production, but they are scrutinized for increased harvest. The result is that they tend to shy away from using harvest to increase water production. Even so, water may be the most precious commodity on Forest Service lands.

SHIFTING TIMBER PRODUCTION

The failure of the national forests to produce much timber is shifting timber production other places. Private industrial harvest in the southern United States now exceeds annual growth for the first time in fifty years. But a major ecological impact comes from the increase in timber production elsewhere in the world. Timber imports into the United States have increased 33 percent since 1990 (Bureau of the Census 2000, 689). This means that some countries perhaps less suited to timber production are providing timber for our consumption. Researchers have shown that by locking up productive timberlands in our own country, we are exporting environmental damage to others (Sohngen, Mendelsohn, and Sedjo 1999). Many wood-exporting countries have little regard for forest health or environmental protections. With less timber production in the United States, the use of wood substitutes is also likely to rise, and production of steel and concrete can be far more environmentally damaging than growing trees (CORRIM 2001). These additional ecological costs, generally ignored by the political operatives, should be a factor in public land-management decisions.

CONCLUSION: WHAT USE FOR PUBLIC LANDS?

Multiple use was once the guiding principle for public land management, and it provides a way to meet the widely divergent demands of the American public. The difficulty arises in determining what the best uses are across such a vast and varied landscape. In recent years, the Forest Service and to a lesser extent the Bureau of Land Management have abandoned multiple use in favor of setting aside vast tracts of public land for minimal or nonuse. This policy misses the mark both economically and ecologically. Some land is certainly better left "untrammeled by man," as Congress described wilderness in 1964. Other areas, however, require hands-on management to treat existing problems or to address future conditions resulting from fire, disease, insects, or human use that could threaten the integrity of the forest. "Our national priority should be environmental stewardship, not environmental protection," says Henry Lamb, executive vice president of the Environmental Conservation Organization.[25] The pendulum of public land-use policy has swung so far toward nonuse that it is harming the environment that nonuse is intended to protect.

NOTES

1. The Conservation Biology Institute and World Wildlife Fund USA (1999) have compiled a protected area database listing numerous federal land classifications by degree of protected status.

2. Proclamations of "conservation" areas have been made by nearly every president since 1906.

3. Natural Resource Conservation Service, WRP Acres by State FY2003, available at http://www.nrcs.usda.gov/programs/wrp/State_Maps_Stats/acres_sm.jpg.

4. *CRP acres seen increasing again in 2003*, Agriculture Online, available at http://www.agriculture.com/default.sph/AgNews.class?FNC=sideBarMore__AMynews_html___49610.

5. *Habitat Conservation Planning: Section 10 of the Endangered Species Act*, US-FWS, available at http://endangered.fws.gov/hcp/HCP_Incidental_Take.pdf.

6. Safe Harbor Agreements for Private Property Owners, USFWS, available at http://northflorida.fws.gov/Documents/FWS safeharborqa.pdf.

7. Bruce Lippke, director, Rural Technology Initiative, Seattle, Washington, telephone interview, August 10, 2000.

8. The Knutson-Vandenberg Act of 1930 and amendments (16 USC 576–576b) allow a portion of timber sale receipts to be retained by the agency for forest restoration, all salvage sale receipts are retained to cover the direct costs of sale preparation and harvest of salvage timber, and 10 percent of the National Forest Fund is retained for trails and road maintenance.

9. Jeff Mann, program analyst, Region 1, U.S. Forest Service, Missoula, Montana, by email, September 14, 2000.

10. Art Johnston, legislative chairperson, Forest Service Council of the National Federation of Federal Employees, Park Falls, Wisconsin, by email, June 26, 2000.

11. Jan Lerum, district ranger, Gallatin National Forest, Bozeman, Montana, personal interview, June 2000.

12. Jeff Mann, telephone interview, September 14, 2000.

13. John Gerritsma, Coconino National Forest, U.S. Forest Service, Region 3, Flagstaff, Arizona, telephone interview, November 3, 2000.

14. Many of the 180 decisions were appealed multiple times.

15. Written communication with Dixie Dies, FOIA Coordinator, USFS, May 12, 2003, Hamilton, Montana.

16. Telephone communication with Ken Gibson, Forest Service Region 1, entomologist, May 27, 2003.

17. Additional data provided by Don McKenzie, Southeast field representative, Wildlife Management Institute, Ward, Arkansas, telephone interview, January 30, 2001.

18. Cathy Stewart, manager and silviculturist, Bitterroot National Forest, Missoula, Montana, personal interviews, October 6 and 13, 1998.

19. The Society of American Foresters, *The Forestry Source*, May 2004, available at http://www.safnet.org/archive/0504_nwfp.cfm. Cited July 11, 2005.

20. Some scientists believe "meteorology and weather are equally important factors" (Ament 1997, 9).

21. Don McKenzie, Southeast representative, the Wildlife Institute, telephone interview, January 30, 2001.

22. Jim Witwer, Trout & Raley PC, Denver, Colorado, letter dated September 19, 1999.

23. See original forest plans.

24. Cliff Reed, information officer, Quabbin Visitor Center, Bekkertown, Massachusetts, telephone interview, August 20, 1998.

25. Henry Lamb, Hollow Rock, Tennessee, by email, April 10, 2001.

Chapter Five

How Much is Enough?

We have seen that the public land agencies are having trouble managing the federal estate. Part of the reason is that the shift away from commodity production (in the Forest Service in particular) has made less money available for forest restoration and rehabilitation. In addition, having so much land set aside in "hands-off" management poses ecological challenges. In spite of these problems, and despite the hefty growth of the federal estate in the past forty years, many politicians and professional environmentalists support further expansion.

A group of environmental organizations, for example, has urged the Forest Service to buy more "sensitive or threatened habitats" (WS 2002, 6).[1] Every year bills are introduced in Congress requesting funds for new land acquisitions. "A major increase in federal funding for land acquisition has long been needed. . . . There is a tremendous backlog in land purchases," says Sierra Club executive director Carl Pope (*San Diego Earth Times*, 1999). The National Parks Conservation Association pleads with Congress to increase funding for the creation of new parks and to expand existing parks.[2] Ron Tipton, a vice president with the National Parks Conservation Association, would like to see more growth in the National Park System and more money for management.[3]

Yet poor federal land stewardship is widely documented. Our national parks have a maintenance backlog of more than $5 billion leaving antiquated sewer systems in need of repair, park roads riddled with potholes, and historical artifacts soaked from rain (GAO 2003b, 1). At least 90 million acres of national forests are at risk of catastrophic wildfire (GAO 2003c, 14). More than 60 percent of our federal grazing lands do not meet environmental objectives (FS 2000e, 32–43).[4] These facts suggest that bigger is not necessarily better for the federal estate.

Stewardship appears to come second after land acquisition. Though billions of dollars are spent each year to manage our federal lands, the public is not getting the benefits of multiple-use, fiscal responsibility, or good resource stewardship. Even valued national treasures are not well cared for. In Yellowstone National Park, sewage seeps into native trout streams. At Gettysburg National Military Park, rain from a leaky roof soaks Civil War relics. At Chaco Cultural National Historical Park, nine ancient Anasazi stone structures are collapsing (Satchell 1999, 2).

Surprisingly, few of our national parks have detailed and comprehensive information on the resources they are supposed to be protecting. James Duffus, director of national resource management issues in the U.S. General Accounting Office, has testified that the National Park Service lacks basic information on the condition of its natural and cultural resources. Identification of the resources is the elemental first step to achieving any scientific understanding or developing procedures for protecting park resources (Sellars 1997, 269). After eight decades of management, a new program was introduced to the park service in 1999. The Natural Resource Challenge was designed to inventory park resources for the first time. By 2007, 64 percent of the park natural resource inventories were complete. The systems performance was rated "moderately effective." Many park natural systems are still not understood sufficiently to determine key parameters for measurement (OMB 2008).

Professionals in varied fields have also questioned the ability of the National Park Service to fulfill its mission of resource protection. Wildlife ecologist Charles Kay of Utah State University has documented the destruction of Yellowstone Park resources by an overpopulation of elk and bison. The result is starvation of thousands of elk, an overgrazed range, the destruction of plant communities, the elimination of critical habitat, and a serious decline in biodiversity (Kay 1997).[5] Ecologist Karl Hess Jr. (1993, 33) reports similar ecological threats from ungulate overpopulation in Rocky Mountain National Park.

Our national forests, too, are damaged and in poor health. Nearly a century of fire suppression has literally changed the structure of many forestlands. At least 90 million acres of federal forest land are at extreme risk to catastrophic wildfire (GAO 2003c, 14). Once-open savannas of ponderosa pine forests are today loaded with debris. Forests are now denser. Their competition for water, nutrients, and sunlight leaves trees sickly and stunted (Fretwell 1999a). Ponderosa pine forests in the Southwest are thirty-one times denser and mixed conifer forests in southern California as much as 74 percent denser than the forests of sixty years ago (Bonnicksen 2001).

The national refuge system, managed by the Fish and Wildlife Service, also shows signs of neglect. After twenty-nine years working in the system,

Gene Hocutt, retired refuge manager, says buildings are in poor condition, dikes are not well maintained, and activities that help maintain wildlife such as planting grass and nesting cover for birds is not adequate (*Discovery News Brief*, December 31, 1999). The Audubon Society says the National Wildlife Refuges are "in dire need of care" (NAS 2001). Worse yet, many Fish and Wildlife Service (FWS) employees feel pressured to present rosier findings than their research may imply (PEER 2005).

These problems have arisen even though the land agencies are spending much more money. Over the last four decades, federal land holdings increased 6 percent (an area the size of Florida). But operating budgets have risen a colossal 278 percent above inflation. This far exceeds both the growth in acreage and in visitation.[6]

It turns out that land management is expensive, even when land is serving purposes of recreation or habitat provision rather than logging or other commodity production. Although the majority of Americans support land conservation, few know what it entails. Conservation is the protection of a natural area so that it may be used for any number of purposes, including recreation, wildlife habitat, or even commodity production. It may require building and maintaining trails, removing timber or woody debris, igniting prescribed burn, or eliminating exotic species. Merely placing land into federal ownership in no way ensures its conservation.

From 1965 to 2002, the Land and Water Conservation Fund (LCWF), a leading source of funds for land acquisition, provided nearly $12.5 billion for acquisition. But the costs of managing the land were $224 billion or 17 times the cost of acquisition! About $10.3 billion was spent in 2002 alone (OMB 2003).

The Congressional Budget Office has gone so far as to suggest a freeze on federal land acquisitions. A 1999 report asserts that "land management agencies should improve their stewardship of the lands they already own before taking on additional management responsibilities." The report goes on to say that "environmental objectives such as habitat protection and access to recreation might be best met by improving management in currently held areas rather than providing minimal management over a larger domain" (Congressional Budget Office 1999, 68).

Similar sentiment resided with the Bush administration. Former Secretary of the Interior Gale Norton has commented on the costs of adding acreage to the federal estate. The administration has made a commitment to find more innovative approaches using public-private partnerships for conservation instead of outright federal land acquisition.[7]

Rather than suffer political punishment because of their economic and ecological deficiencies, the federal land agencies are rewarded with more land being placed under their control. Since 1960, the major federal land agencies have added more than 56,000 square miles to their holdings, giving them control of more than 1 million square miles or more than one-fourth of the land area of the United States.

PROPELLING GROWTH

The federal government acquires land in a variety ways. The Land and Water Conservation Fund (LWCF), established in 1964, is the largest source of federal funding for land conservation. Bankrolled primarily by lease payments from offshore oil and gas drilling, its purpose is to assure citizens access to quality outdoor public recreation. Congress must appropriate the funds, with a limitation of $900 million annually. Half is to be spent for federal land acquisition and half for state grant programs. In reality, the average appropriation has been about $100 million a year.

Even without full funding of the Land and Water Conservation Fund, it has bankrolled an expansion of the federal estate. The four federal land agencies—the Bureau of Land Management (BLM), U.S. Fish and Wildlife Service (FWS), U.S. Forest Service (FS), and National Park Service (NPS)—have added 35.8 million acres to their domain since 1960 (see table 5.1). This growth has averaged 988,000 acres each year, which is the equivalent of adding an area greater than the size of Rhode Island to the federal estate every year.

Federal lands increased more than 7 million acres in the 1990s alone. The National Park Service added 3.4 million acres and twenty-five new units.[8] The national refuge system under the Fish and Wildlife Service added twenty-four new units, incorporating 3 million new acres. The Forest Service expanded its boundaries by 1.8 million acres. Federal land agencies now control an area more than six times the size of California. Found mostly in the West and Alaska, these lands total 614 million acres.

Table 5.1.   Federal Land Acreage (millions of acres)

Agency	1960	2002	Change	Percent Change
BLM	352.2	242.0	(110.1)*	(31%)
FWS	16.0	95.5	79.4	495%
FS	184.7	192.5	7.8	4%
NPS	25.7	84.2	58.7	228%
Total	578.6	614.4	35.8	6%

*Ten million acres were submerged lands in Alaska that were removed from the BLM land base estimates. The remaining acres were transferred to other federal agencies under the Alaska National Interest Lands Conservation Act.

But that is not all the land under federal control. The Department of Defense claims an additional 28 million acres, with another 2 million under the Department of Energy.[9] The Bureau of Reclamation controls 8.5 million acres.[10] There are 11.7 million acres under the control of the U.S. Army Corps of Engineers (2000). The Conservation Reserve Program, run by the Department of Agriculture (USDA), controls 34 million acres, although ownership remains in private hands.[11] Finally, the Wetlands Reserve Program, a joint project of the Fish and Wildlife Service and the USDA, manages about 1.5 million acres.[12] When the acreage from these agencies is added to that already controlled by our land management agencies, the total comes to more than 700 million acres, or one-third of the nation, under federal control. And even this is not a complete accounting.[13]

In addition to federal control, state and local governments own and manage land. It is estimated that nearly 200 million acres of land is managed by state governments, with an additional 200 million acres of subsurface mineral rights and lands under navigable waterways.

Although a variety of federal agencies and funding mechanisms have been involved in the expansion of the federal estate, the federal side of LWCF funding has propelled land acquisition for forty years. Funds provided to the states can be used for land acquisition but also for a wide variety of other undertakings related to recreation such as trail maintenance, wildlife habitat enhancement, and even facility construction. LWCF matches funds for up to 50 percent of the cost of these projects.

Quite different rules apply to the use of LWCF funds on federal lands. Funds are restricted to land and water acquisition unless otherwise appropriated by Congress.[14] No money is available for the improvement, restoration, or management of any federal lands (Americans for Our Heritage and Recreation 2000, 9).

A period of rapid federal land acquisition followed the fund's creation. From 1965 to 1980, Congress appropriated approximately $6.2 billion in LWCF funds for federal land acquisition and another $6.9 billion for state programs.[15] Approximately 69 percent of the funds were earmarked for acquisition of national park land. The result was a jump in the National Park Service's average annual growth rate from .2 percent to 10 percent and the addition of six new units per year, doubling the pace of previous decades. It was during this time that the moniker "park-of-the-month program" was bestowed on the National Park Service.

Between 1965 and 1980, nearly 90 percent of the funds available from the LWCF were appropriated for conservation purposes such as those indicated above. Since 1980, however, Congress has appropriated 68 percent of the funds for purposes unrelated to conservation such as paying down the national debt.[16] During the 1981 to 2002 period, only 32 percent of the funds available were appropriated to the LWCF with $6.3 billion going for federal acquisitions, and $1.6 billion for state programs.

A number of recent legislative proposals would guarantee full funding of the LWCF. The Conservation and Reinvestment Act (CARA) nearly passed Congress in 1999 and continues to reappear in similar form year after year. CARA would have provided nearly $1 billion annually for federal and state land acquisition programs over a fifteen-year period. Bill supporters often tout that the money is for "resource protection," but only a small portion of the funds is available for land management. Instead, the bill proposes to add more acreage to an already fraying federal estate.

With the proposals appearing before Congress, it is likely that LWCF will once again be providing the bulk of the funds needed for an accelerated land acquisition program. Indeed, in 2002, the Bush administration fully funded the LWCF programs for the first time in twenty-five years, though LWCF funding declined throughout the remaining years of the administration (CRS 2006). In addition, President Bush diverted a portion of the federal acquisition funds toward private landowner incentives, none of the proposals to increase conservation funding attempted to address growing management and maintenance problems.[17] The Bush administration did allocate other funds, not from the LWCF, to help address that maintenance backlog.

BROKERING LAND ACQUISITIONS

Private land trusts are actively working to increase federal land holdings. In many cases, these trusts act like real estate agents for the federal government. They negotiate land sales, hold options on land until federal money is available, and purchase and transfer lands. When land passes to the federal government, so do the accompanying management costs and responsibilities. This makes transfers to the federal government attractive to land trusts; once the land is in government hands, the trust is unencumbered by future obligations to maintain it.

America's three largest land trusts, the Nature Conservancy, the Conservation Fund, and the Trust for Public Land, transferred over 1 million acres of land to the federal government during the thirty-year period between 1964 and 1994 (GAO 1996, 42). The Nature Conservancy alone has transferred nearly 1 million acres of land to the federal government since its start in 1951.[18] (This number, however, represents less than 10 percent of the 12 million acres that the group reports to have conserved in North America.)

Nearly 40 percent of the acreage that local and regional trusts report as being protected has been transferred to a public agency (LTA 2000).[19] Yet the legal transfer of ownership from private to federal does not constitute conservation. Considering the federal government's track record for land stewardship, the protection of these lands could and should be questioned.

Trusts often prefer not to own lands because they recognize that management is costly. The Rocky Mountain Elk Foundation (2000), for example, rarely retains ownership, but donates or resells acquired habitat to a state or federal agency that will be responsible for its management. Without question, land trusts promote increased federal land ownership.

The availability of funds for federal land acquisition encourages private groups with their own goals to identify land that could be added to the federal estate. The more money that is available, the greater the incentive for land trusts to act as federal land agents. Brokering land deals for the federal government is a low-cost way for private trusts to achieve their conservation goals—assuming, of course, that federal management is sufficient to meet those goals.

Current trends in federal conservation funding show that the availability of federal dollars for private conservation groups is increasing.[20] Acts such as the proposed CARE act of 2003 (S. 476), would further exacerbate the situation. New incentives for charitable giving were proposed that would exempt from taxes 25 percent of the profits from the sale of land to government agencies or nonprofit conservation groups. Benefits of this subsidy, presumably for the giver, would encourage the transfer of land from private to public entities. Such bills encourage land to be sold at a discounted rate to federal agencies or to conservation groups who turn around and sell to federal agencies.

The cost of using land trusts as agents is an area that deserves further exploration. In some cases, federal land agencies have paid land trusts too much. In 1992 and again in 1999, the Inspector General reported that the government's interests were not adequately protected in dealing with nonprofit organizations for land acquisition (USDI 1992, 5; 1999, 3).

Though claiming no net profit when transferring land to the federal government, land trusts do sometimes make a profit in addition to a service fee, which is comparable to the commission paid to a real estate agent. Between fiscal years 1995 and 1997, the government reviewed twenty-one transactions between the National Park Service and nonprofit organizations. For the land conveyed, the National Park Service paid $3 million more than the nonprofits had paid (USDI 1999, 17). But not all private-public transfers generate a cash return. Land trusts also donate land to the federal government and sell it below cost.

When land trusts do transfer land to the federal government, they add that acreage to their tally of protected lands while avoiding all the expenses associated with managing the land. The government, already contending with millions of acres of land in poor condition, assumes even more liability. Thus, trusts that transfer lands to federal agencies that have demonstrated poor stewardship may in fact be failing to fulfill their mission of land conservation.

The high costs of conservation are precisely the reason that many private groups shy away from fee-simple landownership. In fact, many state agencies and private groups turn down land donations that do not include adequate funds for management. To ensure the land's long-term protection, some conservation groups have sought new approaches that support the land's productive use such as the Nature Conservancy's working lands, guided resource development, and user fees. Many Conservancy lands not only protect critical species and their habitat but also continue to make productive use of the land, allowing the revenues earned from activities such as cattle grazing and recreation to help support expanded conservation efforts. The federal government, on the other hand, is obtaining additional acreage with no additional funds for management and no determination of its conservation value.

OUT-COMPETING PRIVATE OWNERS

As more lands are placed under government reign or granted tax-exempt status and subsidies, it becomes harder for private landowners to compete. Why aren't there more private campgrounds and youth hostels? Why aren't more hunting, hiking, and camping available on private lands? The provision of federal recreation at below-market prices takes consumers away from private entrepreneurs who must pay the full cost of their business.

Rather than lose money providing scenic landscapes where people can hike and sightsee, private recreation providers gravitate toward alternative kinds of recreation: theme parks, amusement centers, and even garish museums displaying odd artifacts. Others abandon recreation opportunities altogether, instead selling land to be developed. Examples of private owners undercut by federal recreation opportunities abound.

- Champion International came head-to-head with government competition in the mid-1990s when the company tried to collect user fees to pay the costs of grooming cross-country ski trails in the Pacific Northwest. Rather than pay the fee, recreationists used adjacent groomed trails on federal lands at lower or no cost. Champion discontinued its recreation program.[21]

- The Nightingale Nordic ski center in Lolo, Montana, once provided professional-quality ski trails on summer grazing ground. Located adjacent to the Lolo National Forest, which provided groomed trails at the low cost of $10 per vehicle for an entire season, made it nearly impossible for a private entrepreneur to compete (Bahls 1990).
- In Kentucky, the owners of caverns close to what is now Mammoth Cave National Park were forced to add distinctive and unusual features to the cave tours in order to stay in business. The private caves, open for public tours since 1927, were unable to compete with the neighboring national park, designated in 1946. Because Mammoth Cave charged fees well below the costs of operation, the private facility added an animal park with an Australian theme to distinguish itself and attract customers (Fretwell 1999b, 7).
- International Paper Company (IP), one of the largest timber producers in the United States, manages its lands differently depending upon the surrounding ownership. As discussed in chapter 3, International Paper has leased land to hunting and camping groups in Arkansas, Louisiana, and Texas (where less than 5 percent of the land is federally owned). In contrast, when IP owned land in the Pacific Northwest, it managed none for recreation. The lands were surrounded by national forest that provided hunting and camping for little to no fee (45 percent of the Pacific Northwest is federally owned). IP could not generate sufficient revenues to cover the costs of providing recreation in the region, so the land was managed solely for timber production without consideration of wildlife and views (Fretwell 1999b, 8).

The increase in public land ownership has discouraged the private provision of recreation amenities and conservation. Private owners cannot compete with free and below-cost recreation on federal lands. Theme parks and subdivisions are likely to earn a greater return than providing outdoor recreation opportunities.

POLITICAL WRANGLING

Entrusting the care of federal lands to politicians has resulted in damages that are both widespread and well documented. It is unlikely that they would make the same decisions on their own private property with their own cash. Few senators would buy acreage without considering management costs. Few representatives would allow their roofs to leak or sewage to run across the front yard.

The problem lies with the incentives. Because federal land managers depend on Congress for their budgets, they are removed from the costs and benefits of their actions. Rather than applying their professional skills to the resources in their charge, managers must spend much their time responding to political pressure, court decisions, and conflicting policy goals, while also trying to blaze a trail through the layers of bureaucratic regulations. Congressional incentives are not in line with resource priorities. They are instead to provide visible benefits for constituents.

Political Budgets

Vying for reelection, congressional representatives gallantly provide funds for local projects—in return for votes. New parkland provided with federal pork and at little cost to locals is sure to please constituents. The cost to other taxpayers and competing programs is unrecognized. Such politically motivated measures can undermine Park Service priorities. Lowell National Historical Park in Massachusetts and the American Industrial Heritage Project in Pennsylvania were both added to the Park Service with goals of economic development more than resource protection. Substantial federal funds helped boost the local economies, but the Park Service budget is now spread more thinly.

The very process by which federal land managers must obtain their budgets from Congress encourages political maneuvering and excessive spending (Fretwell 1998, 3–4). For example, Glacier National Park's popular Going-to-the-Sun Road is a marvel to engineers because it has not yet succumbed to the force of gravity. Melting snow is washing away the foundation, leaving voids and two-inch cracks in the pavement (*Wall Street Journal*, November 12, 1999). In the early 1990s, park managers requested funds for road repair and visitor center restoration to protect park resources and visitor safety. As previously noted, decision makers in Washington, some 2,000 miles away, instead appropriated over $3 million earmarked for restoration of a backcountry chalet system used by fewer than 1 percent of park visitors (*USA Today*, December 15, 1997).[22] Montana's congressional delegates succumbed to special interests to renovate the chalets.

Safety concerns about the historic road have since aroused congressional interest. In a typical crisis-mode response, the Park Service was allocated $1 million in 1999 to assess the repairs necessary to rehabilitate the highway. Emergency funding to the tune of $5.1 million followed, enabling the road to remain open and relatively safe for visitors. Six years later a nearly decade-long comprehensive rehabilitation program was begun to repair the road.[23] The road is in such disrepair that it has become a major challenge to restore it without complete closure during peak season. Only a meager portion of the $2 million required annually to maintain the road in its current degraded condition is available in budget appropriations. Even priority-one fixes, those of major safety concern, take three or more years to complete.[24]

Though not as dire, a similar story can be told of Yellowstone's degraded road system. Heavy summer use and frigid winters take a toll on Yellowstone's 310 miles of road. The roads were designed to last fifty years or more when provided with annual maintenance costing $3 to $5 million. But maintenance funds find low priority in Congress, reducing the usable road life closer to twenty-five years. At an expense of about $1 million per mile to rebuild, taxpayers will pay an additional $100 million to rebuild the road versus maintain it.[25] Perhaps this amounts to pennies in the barrel relative to the overall federal budget, but the millions add up quickly if all park system roads are considered.

Government assets in general receive poor care, not just environmental resources. Budgets providing meager funds for maintenance and repairs are typical for military bases and public buses. Rational behavior shows why this is so. Public officials cannot reap reward from public investment. Investment benefits occur in the future, often long after public officials have left office. No personal benefits are realized because they do not own the assets. Constituents demand immediate benefits, thus reinforcing the short-term outlook. Few taxpayers support decisions involving present payment for future benefit. It can be years before forgone maintenance expenditures are readily visible. The fact that Yellowstone's roads are not maintained annually will not burden taxpayers for twenty-five years or more. Hence, projects with immediate and visible benefits that defer costs into the future are favored (Stroup and Goodman 1992, 435).

The same holds true for much of the infrastructure across the nation. Multiple studies have shown the tendency of politicians to postpone maintenance spending (see Stroup and Goodman 1992). Deferred maintenance for the Department of Defense exceeds $11 billion. According to Defense Secretary Donald Rumsfield, "systematic under-investment [has gone on] far too long."[26] It will take years and significant investment to bring military facilities back to par. Comparing public to private incentives, a study of mass transit vehicles showed that private fleets had longer in-service lives and nearly double the resale value of similar public buses (Stroup and Goodman 1992, 440). Unlike public officials, private owners benefit from protecting the long-term asset value.

Postponing maintenance expenditures frees finances for current consumption while reducing the value of the assets and making future repairs more costly. Public officials allocate budgets between current staff, new facilities, day-to-day operations, and maintenance. Because current citizens elect them, they direct the bulk of appropriations to current services that provide immediate benefit and defer less visible costs into the future.

CONCLUSION: FEDERAL MANAGEMENT
DOES NOT OBLIGE CONSERVATION

Land conservation is not accomplished by casting the net of federal owner-ship ever wider. If the goal is to protect watersheds, improve forest health, enhance wildlife habitat, increase recreational opportunities, and so on, our federal land agencies must be reformed. Conservation comes at a high cost, and playing politics in Washington to bolster agency budgets is not the solution. Federal land-management policies should be changed to provide incentives for land conservation free of federal strings. Private groups and individuals should be encouraged to play a larger role in land conservation without competition from federally subsidized sites.

NOTES

1. The Conservation and Reinvestment Act in 1999, introduced by representative Don Young (R-AK) and Senator Frank Murkowski, and Resources 2000, proposed by Senator Barbara Boxer (D-CA) and Representative George Miller (D-CA), both would have fully funded federal land acquisitions under the LWCF in the amount of $450 million annually.

2. National Parks Conservation Association, "Wildlife Protection," available at http://www.npca.org/wildlife_protection/biodiversity/report.

3. Personal conversation, Ron Tipton, Vice President for Park Resource Protection Programs, National Parks Conservation Association, September 13, 1999, Washington, D.C.

4. It is assumed that BLM lands in mid- and early-seral condition do not meet plan objectives. The existing plant communities in these conditions contain less than 50 percent of the potential natural community.

5. The introduction of wolves into the Yellowstone ecosystem in 1996 is beginning to resolve the problem of too many elk in Yellowstone.

6. These figures include total outlays less construction and acquisition for the Forest Service, the Fish and Wildlife Service, the Bureau of Land Management, and the National Park Service as provided by OMB 2003.

7. Statement of Gale A. Norton, Secretary of the Interior before the Senate Committee on Natural Resources on the 2004 President's Budget Request, February 11, 2003, available at http://www.doi.gov/secretary/speeches/senatestatement.htm.

8. History, National Park Service, available at www.cr.nps.gov/history/hisnps/NPSHistory/timeline.htm. Additional units include the Franklin Delano Roosevelt Memorial in Washington. Authorized in 1959, it was not completed and designated until 1997.

9. Data provided electronically by Carol Anadale, Real Property and Policy, General Services Administration, March 6, 2003.

10. Telephone conversation with Stan Seigal, Bureau of Reclamation, Realty Office, Washington, D.C., March 1, 2000.

11. Created under the Food Security Act of 1985, Title XII, the Conservation Reserve Program provides financial payment to farmers and ranchers to enroll in contracts of ten to fifteen years to retire land from agricultural production. As of December 2002, 33.95 million acres were under contract. Conservation Reserve Program, monthly summary, available at www.fsa.usda.gov/dafp/cepd/stats/dec2002.pdf.

12. Initiated under the 1990 Food, Agriculture, Conservation, and Trade Act and revised in 1996, the Wetlands Reserve Program purchases permanent easements, thirty-year easements, and cost-share agreements to restore wetlands mostly converted to cropland. Natural Resource Conservation Service, WRP Acres by State FY2003, available at http://www.nrcs.usda.gov/programs/wrp/State_Maps_Stats/acres_sm.jpg.

13. This tally does not include lands controlled by the Bureau of Indian Affairs, United States Post Office, and other unlisted agencies.

14. Some federal funds have been used for nonacquisition but related projects since 1998.

15. Figures are in 2000 dollars adjusted for inflation.

16. Data provided by David Whiteman, Congressional Research Service, March 3, 1997; Zinn (1998); CRS report 97–792; and FY 2002 Budget of the United States, available at http://w3.access.gpo.gov/usbudget/fy2002/pdf/budget.pdf. Figures are for the 1981–2002 period.

17. The Landowner Incentive Program and Private Stewardship Grant Program were provided $60 million in FY 2002 for private conservation activities to encourage easement acquisitions over fee simple.

18. Telephone conversation, Jon Schwedler, Member Relations Assistant, Nature Conservancy, Arlington, Virginia, September 28, 1999.

19. As defined by the Land Trust Alliance, protected lands include those transferred to public agencies as well as those with no management restrictions other than limited development.

20. DOI budgets, various years, available at www.doi.gov/budgets.

21. Telephone communication with Jack Ward, Champion International, June 24, 1998.

22. See also Leal and Fretwell (1997) and Fretwell (1999b).

23. Glacier National Park Going-to-the-Sun Road project information, available at www.nps.gov/glac/gtsr/advisory/projinfo.htm.

24. *Missoulian*, Restoring the Road Special, available at www.missoulian.com/specials/sunroad/sunroad7.html.

25. Personal communication with Don Striker, former Yellowstone National Park comptroller, October 15, 2001.

26. U.S. Department of the State, International Information Programs, Excerpts: Rumsfield Says 20th Century U.S. Military Needs Fixing, June 28, 2001, available at http://usinfo.state.gov/topical/pol/arms/stories/01062802.htm.

Chapter Six

Understanding Incentives

This book has shown that federal land management is failing to protect many of the nation's most valued lands and resources. The infrastructure in national parks and at cultural and historic sites is crumbling from inadequate maintenance. Wildlife habitat on the federal estate is being destroyed by overgrazing and catastrophic wildfire. Forests are becoming overly dense and more homogeneous. In many cases, the condition of the natural resources on the federal estate is simply unknown because public officials have not had the time or staff to inventory them and research their status.

Before developing alternatives for reform, it is necessary to understand why federal lands have reached this state. Inefficiencies in government, like those in the private sector, stem from the incentives that face decision makers. The purpose of this chapter is to definitively explain just how those incentives affect behavior and to build an understanding of why incentives in the public and private sectors lead to varied outcomes. Typical incentives and their evolution for the private sector are outlined—good and bad—followed by the same for the government sector. The intent is to acknowledge why the public lands are managed as they are, and to realize how they might be improved through the introduction of different incentives.

PRIVATE SECTOR INCENTIVES

The private sector is a complex system full of a multiplicity of forms, from small businesses to giant corporations and including nonprofit organizations and, of course, individuals. At any point in time, there are Enrons and Tycos (companies that took advantage of their employees and stockholders), just as there are companies like Whole Foods Markets (companies that make good profits while also ranking high on lists of good places to work).

Understanding the incentives in the private sector is valuable because most of our activity in this country (and in the rest of the world) is conducted by the private sector. That is, our homes, food, clothing, travel, and even much of our recreation operates under a system of private decision-making. For the most part, this works well and the incentives have something to teach us. At the same time, it must be recognized that the private sector has flaws that should be avoided.

This chapter will bring to light the incentives that face private managers, especially private land managers, in order to make comparisons with the public land agencies that are the topic of this book. At the outset, however, it must be recognized that relatively few land managers in the private sector manage parcels of land that are as extensive as the stretches of national forest or federal grasslands in the western United States. The broad expanses of federal land put a crimp in at least one area of private sector land management—recreation. A lot of federal land is open to the public for little or no payment (access to most forests, even with the recreation fee program, is free). This means that fewer people will go to private land for recreation. The private landowner has to charge fees that cover the costs of management, but the federal government does not. The difficulty of competing with the federal government explains why there are not more Kampgrounds of America or Hawk Mountain Sanctuaries around the country.

Aside from that fact, the major obvious difference between private and public owners and managers is that private owners have clearer goals. Businesses have a profit motive; individuals have an incentive to retain or increase the value of what they own. The corollary is that private owners bear the loss of value when the worth of their assets decreases.

Suppose, for example, that you let the roof of your house leak, the walls crumble, the garden go to seed, and the trees in your yard wither. Your home will lose some of its value. As the owner, you will be the one to experience that financial loss. An owner of property who allows the property to deteriorate will pay the cost of that deterioration through a decline in the value of the land. On the bright side, if you keep the roof and the walls and the yard in good shape, the value of your home will be higher.

Of course, we all know some people who do not bother to maintain their homes and we know of businesses that have poorly run operations that sometimes end in bankruptcy. We know that not all landowners want to protect land for conservation—many, for example, may prefer to use it for growing trees that will be cut down and sold, for farming, or for a housing development.

As we will see below, however, even profit-oriented owners have an incentive to consider conservation values. And when people do let their houses or their businesses deteriorate, it is likely that someone else will buy the assets to enhance their value. Unlike the government sector, there are many different private owners and there is frequent changeover of hands. Those who neglect their property open up opportunities for those who see potential value in it. A house that is not kept up may become a "fixer-upper" that another family is able to afford. If others perceive that a poorly managed property can be put to a greater valued use, they may try to acquire it and earn a return. In contrast, most government ownership is permanent. Poor management can go on for a very long time because there is no convenient system for shifting land to more responsible managers or higher-valued uses.

Just as a homeowner tries to maintain both the present and future value of a home, a large landowner benefits from maintaining the value of the land. Ranchers, for example, will manage their rangelands to ensure sufficient forage for current livestock without depleting the range for future use. They recognize that overgrazing their land today will result in lower returns in the future. Taking into account current and potential future revenues, they determine the appropriate number of livestock for the range. (This clear connection between good stewardship and profit over time, by the way, is weakened when the land the ranchers are using is public.)

If returns to livestock production fall, ranchers may seek alternative ways of earning money from their land. Ranchers may decide that the land will earn more if it is sold for homes or "ranchettes." Certainly, this happens, especially near growing urban areas, where the demand for new homes may exceed the value of traditional ranching.

But there are other options for the owner of grassland. The owners of the Flynn Ranch in southwestern Montana, for example, acted creatively when returns from livestock were low. They enhanced the wildlife habitat on the property so that they could offer guided elk hunts for a fee. Ranch managers thinned the forest around the grassland because lower forest density encourages new growth of grass, increasing forage for elk and other wildlife. The Flynns are able to keep their ranch intact, while improving the habitat for wild animals and giving hunters the chance to hunt for trophy elk.

Just east of the Flynn ranch, another family has improved its financial returns by improving the environment on its ranch. Two spring creeks meander across the Milesnicks' ranch. For years, they allowed fishermen free access. By the late 1990s, public use of the creeks exceeded 1,500 visitors a year, which together with the effects of grazing was degrading the creeks. Concerned about the state of the stream, the Milesnicks began a $70,000 reclamation project. They removed sediment, laid rocks, planted vegetation, and channeled water to create spawning areas for trout. They fenced the cattle away from the stream banks, but also created cattle crossings by lining sections of the streams with rocks. Now they limit access to six fishers a day and charge a $50 rod fee, bringing the number of visitors to about 600 a year (Kumlien 2002, 11). The new system provides finances for future restoration, protects the fishery, and compensates the Milesnicks for their service to the public and the resource.

Even for a large timber company, harvesting timber is not the only way to use land, as illustrated by International Paper (IP), discussed in chapter 3. IP is a publicly held forest products corporation that produces timber, lumber, paper, and packaging. Though now transforming its focus to processing instead of wood products production, IP was once the largest forestland owner in the United States, managing over 10 million acres. IP was recognized as a careful steward, ensuring that timber stands were sufficient for harvest well into the future. IP found it could increase profits through quality land stewardship and wildlife habitat enhancement. To bring in recreation revenues, its managers logged less in some places, kept trees as buffers next to streams, and created protective wildlife corridors. One reason that IP was able to profitably lease its land for recreation was that its properties in the Southeast were not surrounded by federally owned land. It did not have to compete with below-cost recreation provided by the federal government.

Some timber companies have found their land to be more valuable for development than for continued timber production. When this is the case, some companies will log the land and sell the property for development. But if conservation values—especially those held by potential customers—are high, the end result can reflect those values.

A new ski and summer resort in Montana, for example, has risen from former timberlands. Realizing the potential values in development versus timber, Plum Creek Timber Company harvested much of the timber in a 25,000-acre area adjacent to Big Sky Ski and Summer Resort. The company then put the land up for sale, with a requirement that the next seller would continue to provide the company's mill in Belgrade, Montana, with timber for years to come.

Even with the logging, the land was valued for its wildlife habitat for elk, moose, bear, and mountain sheep. Competing for the land against the Nature Conservancy, three private partners acquired the 25,000-acre parcel with a goal to develop it and a philosophy to "listen to the land" (Moonlight Basin 2006). The result was Moonlight Basin, a residential and ski resort, with a densely developed section near skiing but with conservation protection that is expected ultimately to cover 80 percent of the land. In just over a decade, the developers have already protected over half the acreage under conservation easements that restrict development density in some areas and prohibit it in others. While Plum Creek Timber Company saw the value in the real estate, the developers saw even greater value in real estate combined with conservation.

In general, private landowners will manage their land to obtain the greatest value from the landscape as they perceive it. In some cases, this means responding to the desires of others for fishing, hunting, or conservation. In others, where the value of development exceeds the value in conservation or agricultural value (and where the two values cannot be combined), development is likely to occur. That is happening around many cities. In California 90,000 acres of land were converted to urban development between 1998 and 2000.[1]

We should not exaggerate the impact of development, however. The footprint of urbanization is still small. Less than 5 percent of the nation's land area has buildings, streets, and other development on it (Hayward 2000, 9). Many landowners—both those in agriculture and new buyers who want a beautiful place to live—want to preserve land in a relatively natural state.

OWNERS AND MANAGERS: MISALIGNED INTERESTS

A private owner has an incentive to maximize the benefits from his or her property, and the Flynns and Milesnicks illustrate how families can preserve and enhance their surroundings while adding to their income. Moonlight Basin illustrates the ability of a partnership to do so. But private ownership is often organized in a more complex way, as illustrated by International Paper. Let us look more carefully at the incentive problems that arise when corporations are formed. Managers must be hired, sometimes many of them, and as a result ownership and management are separated. A corporation explicitly separates management and ownership into two distinct functions (Hessen 1993, 563). Like the owner, the manager has an incentive to maximize his or her personal gain, but maximizing the manager's benefits may not be the same as acting in the owner's best interests.

This problem is called the "principal-agent" problem in economics and business. The principal is the owner and the agent is the manager. Because of this disparity between the desires of the hired manager (who could be a well-paid chief executive officer) and the owners (who could be stockholders), a contract or agreement is important. Such a contract specifies duties and compensation, with the goal of influencing the managers to act in the interest of the owners. (Jensen and Meckling 1976, 4).

A great deal of time and effort is spent throughout the private sector attempting to write good contracts. For example, a farm manager paid on an hourly basis may have less interest in maximizing the value of the crops than he or she would if the pay came from a percentage of the crops produced. A proper contract or understanding helps to align the interests of the two parties.

The problem of monitoring arises when the owner and manager are different people. A homeowner can be sure that the roofer he or she hires is doing a good job when the two are working side by side. If the owner is offsite, however, it is more difficult to ensure efficient, quality workmanship; and the more distant the owner, the more costly the monitoring. Again, the contract is an issue: If the roofer is paid by the hour, the project may be slow to reach completion. Paying on the basis of the number of shingles laid will encourage speed but perhaps hinder quality application. The purpose of a contract is to define the work to be performed and method of accountability to the satisfaction of both parties (see Eggertsson 1990, 89).

These relationships become more difficult as the business becomes larger. Even with large corporations, however, the owners—shareholders—can have a direct impact on the way a company is managed.

Typically, shareholders are outside investors who will only invest if they believe that the company will earn a profit. Thus the current value of a corporation depends on the shareholders' anticipation of future profits. If shareholders perceive poor management, they can get out by selling their shares—and perhaps investing in companies that appear to have a better future. The shareholders help themselves this way, but they also influence management. If a lot of shareholders perceive a problem, many will sell, and the price—and thus value—of the company will go down. Lowering the value of the corporation (the value of the owners' property) is the last thing the remaining shareholders want, and the managers know that they need to maintain or increase the value of the corporation for the sake of their job security and reputation.

MISSING PRIVATE INCENTIVES

Certainly, there are flaws in the marketplace. Some of them stem from this separation between owners and managers. Another problem that creeps up is whether the market can provide a "public good." To economists, a public good has a specific meaning, somewhat different from our general use of the word as something provided by the public sector that benefits the general public. Economists define a public good as something that benefits the general public when at the same time it is difficult or impossible to exclude people from those benefits. Because of this characteristic, the private sector may not provide these public goods or a sufficient amount of them because producers of the benefit may not be adequately compensated.

For example, private owners—motivated by profit—can provide attractive, uncrowded land for recreation, as they do through campgrounds and parks. But will the private sector provide land that provides other attributes as well? Wilderness areas and other protected lands give us much more than recreation. They provide habitat for fauna and flora. They are sites for scientific research. They help maintain quality watersheds. They offer opportunities for spiritual reflection, even from afar.[2] Wallace Stegner, the distinguished author, called America's wilderness lands "an intangible and spiritual resource" (Stegner 1960).

These attributes are not necessarily ones that someone is willing to pay for—or it simply may be impossible to collect the funds to support them. Wilderness may be valuable for the public through providing clean drinking water in cities or medical advances based on scientific research, but people consume these benefits without physically visiting the wilderness. When no visit is made, collecting payment is nearly impossible.

Some people will pay voluntarily, however. For example, individuals interested in protecting wildlife habitat may donate money that organizations such as the Nature Conservancy can use to acquire and manage sensitive lands. But others will not, and the private sector cannot force people to pay for them. Hence, many economists believe that markets fail to protect the desired amount of habitat (Krutilla 1967, 782).

Is this underprovision of habitat a permanent or temporary situation? Over time, some public goods may be increasingly provided privately. Today, as the demand for natural amenities rises, more groups are protecting land that provides the public goods of wildlife habitat, clean watersheds, and scientific research. In addition to the many individuals and businesses that protect land for conservation (see Anderson and Leal, 1997), a fast-growing land trust movement is acquiring land or use rights on land for conservation purposes.

EVOLVING PRIVATE INCENTIVES

Let's consider how conservation easements are helping to correct what seemed to be a market failure. Suppose that a farm on the edge of a growing suburb provides open space, scenic views, and wildlife habitat. Many citizens appreciate these attributes of the farm but few are willing to individually pay for them, and collecting funds from them would be awkward if not impossible.

Thus, the farm is providing public goods. The landowner doesn't receive any financial reward by providing them, so he or she may sell out once the value of development exceeds the productivity of the farm.

Conservation easements can change the landowner incentives. The land remains private, but the owner may give up some rights to the land, such as the right to build a housing development or to harvest timber. These rights may be sold or donated to a public agency, a charitable trust, or a land trust. If the landowner sells the rights, the land will probably be worth less, but the landowner is compensated for the rights.[3] If the development rights are donated, the owner can be compensated through tax benefits. Indeed, the use of conservation easements is growing in large part because of these and other tax benefits (Parker 2005). Because the easements reduce taxes, other taxpayers are in effect helping the landowner pay for the conservation easement.

Setting aside land as a conservation easement is not simple. The land must have historic significance, special natural habitat attributes, scenic views, or be suitable for public outdoor recreation or education.[4] To qualify as a charitable donation under federal tax law, it must be preserved in perpetuity—forever. And because of the financial incentives that conservation easements provide to property owners, it is possible that owners will seek easements for their tax benefits rather than their conservation value.

Although they help supply the public good benefits of open space and other environmental goods desired by the public, the incentives provided by conservation easements are not perfect either. Conservation easements remove specific land uses from the market forever. Over the short term, this can distort local real estate markets. Over the long-term the consequences can be even more negative.

The experience of the township of Old Mission Peninsula in northern Michigan illustrates the short-term distortion. In an effort to restrain development and retain open space, the township approved a property tax in 1996 to fund the purchase of development rights through conservation easements. As the township established easements, it reduced the amount of land available for development. The remaining lots with development rights shot up in value. While the costs of development rights increased by one-third, the price of unrestricted land doubled.[5] Construction and development became more profitable and gave farmers an even greater incentive to sell their land to developers (Davis 1999). The goal was to maintain the agricultural "feel" of the landscape. But the result was to expedite development on unrestricted land and to price many people out of the market.

The long-term concern is twofold. First, the same process that occurred in Old Mission Peninsula—the pressure to develop more land—can occur over a long time period. Although more open space may be protected, some of the land may be more valuable for protection than other parcels. Continuing to expand the protected zone comes at the cost of increasing the value of development on unprotected lands. This encourages more development there, but at higher and higher prices.

Second, needs and values evolve over time. Land that is protected today may have little value for scenic beauty or environmental amenities fifty years hence. But because conservation easements are perpetual, a land trust cannot sell one easement in order to obtain another easement that has greater conservation value. Instead, more and more land must be set aside.

Imagine a future where agricultural yields continue to increase, so less cropland in a particular area is required to produce the same amount of product. Cropland that is under a conservation easement for agricultural use might better serve as a recreational park or forestland habitat, but the easement is perpetual. IRS rules allow for conservation easements to be extinguished if changing conditions make them "impractical or impossible," but this must be determined by the courts (Parker 2005, 14). The cost to change conservation easements is high.

To put this in perspective, recall that in the East much of the land that was once farmland has reverted to forest over the past 100 years or so as farming moved to the Midwest. Under perpetual conservation easements, land remains in the use that the current generation defines. Had conservation easements been used to protect farming, what are now eastern forests would be subsidized farmland. The conservation-easement approach will limit the future use of millions of acres of land, even though advances in science and technology may make these protections obsolete.

In spite of these drawbacks, however, conservation easements represent an active market for land use on private land, aided by tax advantages.

The federal government also has some direct incentive programs to encourage private landowners to favor conservation and wildlife. One, the Conservation Reserve Program (CRP), provides federal dollars to change the incentives for private landowners. Funded by the Department of Agriculture the CRP pays farmers to leave lands fallow or convert cropland from production to native cover. The primary goal of the CRP, which began in 1985, was to reduce soil erosion and decrease the production of commodities that were in oversupply. Receiving about $50 per acre, over 400,000 farmers have nearly 36 million acres set aside under CRP.[6]

The program is controversial for a number of reasons. It can be debated, for example, whether the program has reduced erosion or total crop output. It has, however, increased wildlife habitat and maintained open space, or at least slowed suburban growth in some areas by raising the value of retaining the land to the farmer (Tschida 2004).[7] Once again we see incentives at work.

Managers who are rewarded for providing wildlife habitat are more likely to effectively manage to achieve wildlife habitat, public or private.

Although some federal programs encourage protection of space for wildlife, others can reduce it. This appears to be the case with the Endangered Species Act. The law, enacted in 1973, aimed at preventing species extinction and recovering species whose populations were declining. The act calls for restrictions on how land is used if it is determined to be suitable habitat for endangered species. The Endangered Species Act gives great power to federal officials to restrict activity on both public and private land in order to protect the habitat of animals listed as threatened or endangered. Private landowners may be prohibited from building, farming, cutting down trees—from any activity that may alter the endangered species habitat. As a result, the act has made endangered species a serious liability to many private property owners.

The unintended consequence is that many landowners do not want to improve habitat for threatened or endangered species. They may not even want anyone to know whether or not they have habitat for threatened or endangered species: The risk of being regulated is greater than any perceived benefits, and the government does not have to provide the landowner with any compensation for the loss of the value of the land.

Even though the disincentives of the Endangered Species Act have been long recognized, Congress has been unable to provide substantial reform. According to Michael Bean of Environmental Defense, who had a hand in writing the act, some landowners are making rational decisions to reduce habitat in order to avoid restrictions on how they can use their land. Says Bean: "increasing in evidence that at least some private land owners are actively managing their land so as to avoid potential endangered species problems . . . not the result of malice toward the environment . . . but fairly rational decisions motivated by a desire to avoid potentially significant economic constraints . . . predictable responses to the familiar perverse incentives that sometimes accompany regulatory programs." (Bean 1994)

The executive branch has introduced a number of new programs to try and change these incentives. The Landowner Incentive Program and the Private Stewardship Grant Program provide federal matching grants to individuals and groups that protect and restore habitat on private lands for species at risk. The Cooperative Endangered Species Conservation Fund provides grants to assist private landowners in protecting candidate, proposed, and listed species and in the development of Habitat Conservation Plans (HCPs) and Safe Harbor Agreements. These are special arrangements by which landowners can avoid the penalties of restricted land use by designating and enhancing habitat areas for endangered species. These arrangements guarantee landowners the right to use their land once they have met specified stipulations. Although

HCPs do not provide landowners with compensation for the loss of value on their land, they reduce the risk of more drastic restrictions. About 42 million acres across the United States are under 675 HCP agreements, and this number is expected to double in the near future (CBB 2008; DOI 2008).

These plans act as an insurance policy for landowners, but these agreements are only nominally voluntary—that is, they are formulated under pressure and are often expensive. Designing and maintaining such plans can cost millions of dollars.

HOW FEDERAL LAND AGENCIES RESPOND

The above overview of the private sector shows that problems can arise when owners are different from managers; that some conservation goals may be different from the goals of landowners; and that some "public goods" are difficult for the private sector to provide. It also reveals that both private organizations and governments can introduce programs that give private landowners incentives to conserve more land or protect more wildlife. Such programs include the purchase of land by a land trust, the use of conservation easements, and federal programs such as stewardship contracts. But other forces, such as the Endangered Species Act, can reduce the incentive to provide wildlife habitat.

Now let us move to federal land managers and their incentives. Understanding federal land management becomes easier when we recognize that the land managers are agents, too, but even farther removed from the principals, the owners of the lands, its citizens. In addition, the ability of the government to require people to pay through taxes changes the incentives of the agents.

With respect to the federal lands, the nation's citizens are comparable to shareholders. Unlike shareholders, however, they cannot sell their shares if they are dissatisfied. Instead, an extensive network of political relationships involving voters, politicians, and bureaucrats determines decisions about land use. To give a brief synopsis of the process, voters elect congressmen, who designate the budgets of agencies, but officials of the executive branch make the actual spending decisions.

There are incentive problems all along the way. To begin with, the voters have little direct impact on the thousands of decisions that congressmen make each year, so they tend to be less informed and less interested than are shareholders. Congressmen, as agents of the voter, have an incentive to take actions that benefit themselves (as evidenced by the $1 million outhouse in the Glacier Park chalet system). Agency officials must use the funds as Congress tells them, even though the appropriations may not address the problems that most concern the agency officials; in addition, agency officials, as agents, have their own incentives that may not be the same as the taxpayers'. Yet it is in the interest of agency heads—the political appointees or bureaucrats—to respond positively to congressional requests. Their reward is to remain in their appointed posts and obtain continually larger budgets. But the resulting actions do not necessarily represent the best interests of the owners, the citizens.

This system has led to the rise of powerful special interests. Although companies are often criticized for short-term thinking, political decisions are often made with even shorter-term considerations in mind (as discussed in chapter 2). Congressmen are elected every two years, senators every six years, and these elected officials must provide visible signs of success if they are to be reelected (Lindsay 1976). In addition, they need sizeable campaign funds, and the constituents most likely to provide the bulk of these funds are those who are most vocal and well organized and who have a direct stake in the outcome of the decisions. The result is many visible actions that look good to the general public at election time satisfy special interests rather than provide for the long-term needs of the general public and the public lands. As has been shown throughout this book, such political pressure can prevail even if the result is not ecologically or economically sound. This short-term management outlook is taken because the management team is rewarded for responding to the chain of command and receives little reward for long-term stewardship of the resources.

Timber management illustrates the operation of highly focused interest groups (Nelson 1994–1995, 348). For example, in the 1950s, logging lobbies had greater political influence than other national forest users. Politicians encouraged the agriculture undersecretary, who oversees the Forest Service, to increase federal timber harvest targets. The undersecretary accomplished this by applying pressure to the chief of the Forest Service. Allowable harvest levels in all national forests rose from 6 billion board feet in 1950 to 11 billion board feet in 1960. Then in 1961, President Kennedy introduced the "Development Program for National Forests," aiming to reach a long-term allowable harvest of 21 billion board feet by 2000 (Fedkiw 1996, 43, 47).

The harvest and terracing in the Bitterroot National Forest in the late 1960s (as discussed in chapter 1) were one result of this political mission. There was no concern for the excessive cost of reforestation or the lessened ecological value of the forest.

Twenty years later, timber harvest in the national forests declined. That reduction was not instigated by the Forest Service in response to changing demands from the landowners, the citizens, nor was it the result of improved science indicating reduced harvest levels could enhance forest health. Rather, the reduction in timber harvest beginning in the early 1990s was largely the result of new forest set-asides required by the courts to provide habitat for the northern spotted owl, an endangered species. The judicial decisions were followed by executive orders under the Antiquities Act restricting activities on millions of acres of land.

Today, the emphasis of the Forest Service is on ecosystem management. This mission resonates better with current American desires and environmental advocacy groups. During the 1990s, Congress was somewhat divided over how to manage public lands—partly because of expensive impacts such as the halting of timber in parts of the Pacific Northwest to protect the northern spotted owl. Environmental groups, however, found that they could sway the president and his political appointees to take action that restricted the use of federal land, keeping millions of acres of forestland roadless and establishing national monuments on large swaths of land. Timber harvest was reduced to less than 3 billion board feet.

In the case of land management, an effort has been made to bring in the views of "the citizens" in the form of public input. Pressured by the courts and encouraged by the National Environmental Policy Act (NEPA), agencies are expected to incorporate public values through the process of public hearings and public comment (Ballard 2002).

But the public has an abundance of differing viewpoints that cannot be condensed into a single vision that can guide public land management. Preservationists would like to see land left untouched by humans, letting nature take its course. Recreation users are divided. Some prefer active management to enhance wildlife habitat, such as tree thinning to improve grizzly migration routes or the creation of meadows to increase forage for elk and deer. Others want roads for access and sightseeing by car, bike, ATV, or snowmobile, and still others want roadless areas for hiking and cross-country skiing. Some groups believe that federal forests should provide timber to nearby mills to help create jobs and fill society's need for wood products; others oppose the harvest of any commercial timber on federal lands. Each group and each individual has a different vision of how the land should be managed. Given all these possible outcomes, is it any wonder that scientific management—the original impetus for the Forest Service—is not the major driver determining public land use?

The federal land agencies are unable to find a compromise that can satisfy such divergent viewpoints. No mechanism exists in government to place a value on these varied land uses or to provide a priority system. The information provided in the marketplace by price signals between producer and consumer is not communicated. No one who looks at government decisions concludes that the government has found the highest-valued mix of resource uses.

The mission of the federal land agencies has become the subject of an ongoing debate among elected officials who are struggling to represent the disparate viewpoints of their constituents. Political influence has resulted in management decisions that promote extremes—highly restricted public land uses, on the one hand, or exploitation, on the other. Quite simply, governments are not good land managers because they lack information, have the wrong incentives, and have a short-term outlook that corresponds to the political election cycle. With open markets and private management, the price system produces a wide variety of products meeting many different consumer demands. With government management only the demands of the most influential are met.

CONCLUSION: INCENTIVES MATTER

This chapter has argued that the problems with federal management lie in the incentives of the managers. Private landowners reap what they sow through the reward of profit and the punishment of loss, but federal land managers receive no financial gain from fiscal responsibility and long-term stewardship. Rather, federal land managers are rewarded for providing immediate benefits to constituents. While the livelihood of private land managers depends on the present and future productivity of the land, the livelihood of federal land mangers depends on the next congressional budget and election cycle. Although we have seen that private incentives are not always perfect, maintaining a close link between principal and agent, owner and manager, helps keep the incentives right. Using this knowledge to adjust the management on our federal lands can help enhance land stewardship and increase value.

NOTES

1. California Department of Conservation, News Room, State's Farmland Disappearing at a Faster Rate, available at http://www.consrv.ca.gov/index/news/2003%20News%20Releases/NR2003-14_Farmland_Conversion_1998-2000.htm.

2. See Krutilla 1967 regarding option value.

3. An easement may also increase the value of land if the protection of surrounding land is valued more than development.

4. As provided by the IRS tax code. The ramifications of tax benefits are further discussed in Bick and Haney 1999 (American Farm Bureau).

5. Telephone communication with Gordon Hayward, Old Mission Peninsula Township Planner, February 9, 2000.

6. USDA Farm Service Agency, Conservation Reserve Program Monthly Summary, October 2005, available at http://www.fsa.usda.gov/dafp/cepd/stats/Oct2005.pdf. Cited November 30, 2000.

7. Available at http://helenair.com/articles/2004/02/02/montana/a08020204_01.txt. Cited February 14, 2006.

Chapter Seven

Prescription for Reform

This book has shown that federal land managers frequently lack the information or the incentives they need to make decisions that protect and enhance our federal lands. This is largely because funding comes from congressional appropriations, often through earmarks for specific projects that further political goals. Because land managers rely on appropriations for their budgets, they must accept these earmarks; but their dependence on appropriations reduces the impact that actual users of the lands, such as park visitors, have on management decisions.

Reestablishing the link between users and managers is vital to any attempts to reform federal land management. Managers, users, taxpayers, and the resources themselves would all benefit. This can be done by incorporating incentives that encourage more long-range stewardship and more local knowledge—incentives that are more like those facing private owners. An array of management arrangements has been proposed to do this. The most extreme proposal suggests the transfer of federal land to private ownership. Transferring federal land to state ownership has also been recommended. Such transfers have been largely rejected, yet it can be useful to examine these propositions for their potential benefits and shortcomings.

Other promising alternatives may be more acceptable to the public. Some federal efforts, usually experimental, have already changed incentives for the better. Current reforms include trust management, user fees, and stewardship contracts. Alternatives that should also be tested include nature leases and possibly some limited form of land-use auctions. No perfect solution exists, but an approach that allows greater flexibility, more local control, innovation, and adaptation is long overdue. This chapter will discuss many options.

TRANSFERRING FEDERAL LANDS:
A THOUGHT-PROVOKING EXERCISE

Privatization has been a worldwide trend over the past fifteen years but it has largely bypassed environmental resources. In the United States, the amount of forest, rangeland, and water under federal control has actually increased. Yet the marketplace can provide environmental amenities, too, just as it does in the transportation, energy, and telecommunications sectors, all of which have experienced some degree of deregulation over the past few decades.

For many it would take an enormous leap of faith to take the management of federal lands out of federal hands. Given this prevailing doubt, proposing such a transformation could be political suicide for political leaders. A Forest Service proposal in 2006 to sell off less than one-tenth of a percent of the agency's land was met with bipartisan criticism. Nonetheless, it is a useful exercise to examine such proposals and the mechanisms that might be used to privatize the federal lands in an equitable manner. Such an exercise reveals the potential benefits from private ownership but also exposes the costs and difficulties that may arise.

Privatization

Just as the homestead acts of the nineteenth century spurred development of the western frontier, a return to private rights could encourage environmental stewardship. The demand for agricultural products encouraged settlers to invest in farming. Today, as pristine land has become more scarce, the demand and willingness to pay for conservation values has increased, encouraging investment in environmental stewardship.

A proposal by Anderson, Smith, and Simmons (1999) offers a blueprint for privatizing the federal lands through "share disbursement," a process to transfer land rights to all citizens. The public is the ultimate beneficiary of this transfer. The goal is to increase public welfare by putting federal lands to the uses that will be most highly valued. Each citizen would be granted equal transferable share certificates redeemable for land at auction.

A federal agency, political officials, or a special committee or trust would define the tracts of land as they should be sold. They might be defined by topography, current classification, or other natural historical boundaries. Tracts would have separable rights for various land uses (e.g., mineral, oil and gas, water, grazing, timber, recreational, wilderness). That is, these specific rights could be offered for sale, or restricted. Tracts and various deed rights would be fully transferable. Rights to holders of documented preexisting claims would be deeded to them, with the right of transferability.

This proposal is similar to the denationalization of industries in the Czech Republic in the early 1990s. Each citizen of the Republic could acquire vouchers that gave rights to bid and purchase shares of the state-owned enterprises that were to be privatized. The scheme successfully privatized about 85 percent of the state's assets (Aggarwal and Harper, 2000). Under the U.S. proposal, the public land vouchers, or share certificates, would be used to privatize the federal estate in a similar way.

Every citizen would receive an equal amount of share certificates and could use them to bid on the federal estate as tracts became available. Over a predetermined period of time, perhaps several decades, tracts of federal land would become available for purchase through bid, with share certificates serving as the currency for the bids. During the auction, citizens or groups could bid for any or all rights that coincided with one or more tracts. Individuals uninterested in participating in the land auction could sell, donate, or bequeath their certificates to any willing receiver. In this way, all citizens could "vote" for their preferred land use through the distribution of their certificates.

A bid could be for all rights as we normally think of as private property, but alternatively it could be for just the rights of access for recreation or livestock grazing. The remaining rights (if they were offered) would be left open for other bidders. More specifics would be required to follow through with such a proposal, of course.

It is interesting to think about how resources would be used under the privatized system compared to the existing system. Rather than devoting resources to political lobbying to determine how public land is used, as is the current practice, interest groups could encourage citizens to sell or donate certificates to their causes. The groups could pool their certificates and bid on land or rights aligned with their goals. Preservation groups, for example, could pool certificates to control rights on lands that they wanted to keep from development. Those who wanted to develop land (if the right was being offered for bid), could pool certificates, too, if they could gain the necessary support.

Once a winner emerged, other groups or individuals with interests in the same tract would have an opportunity to contract with the winning bidder. If the highest bidder on a specified tract was a preservation group, for example, parties interested in timber harvest or mining on that tract would have to negotiate for use rights with the new owner. The preservation group could obtain funds by devoting a small part of its land to that use; alternatively, it could turn down such bids and keep the rights (mining rights, say) and simply not use them.

An anti-mining group could use certificates to purchase subsurface rights in order to prevent another group from mining on that land. Likewise, mining companies could use certificates to purchase the subsurface rights on a tract to mine, although they would have to contract with deeded surface rights holders or purchase a combination of subsurface and surface rights. Thus, if one party was outcompeted, it could still negotiate with the winning bidder.

The new owners would be accountable for any harm they did to others. For example, loggers who purchased the rights and intended to harvest would be liable for any environmental or water quality degradation that might affect surrounding tract owners. Presumably this could be settled through the doctrine of common law (where owners are liable for direct harm caused to others) or bonding (a government requirement that companies set aside money for compensation if they cause direct harm to others). Similarly, if a preservation group purchased timber rights on an overly dense, fire-prone tract of forest and stopped logging, the tract and those surrounding it might be at undue risk of wildfire. The group would be liable for effects on surrounding right holders.

One risk of the proposal is its potential for breaking up contiguous landscapes that provide critical corridors for wildlife, recreation, and other amenities. One way to address this is for some tracts to be sold only with predetermined conditions, such as specifying only certain kinds of land uses or requiring that the tract be a minimum size. Such restrictions would make the land less affordable but might help conserve critical habitat.

This proposal does not address the concern that some conservation benefits are hard to capture in the marketplace. To illustrate this, consider that no one may be willing to invest in the cost of protecting the habitat of the Tobusch fishhook, an endangered plant. This may be true even if the Tobusch fishhook is a vital species that other animals depend upon. Although many would agree that allowing the extinction of species is unappealing, few are willing to invest in saving the lesser-known species. Yet, as this book has shown, it is not clear that the federal government does a better job of providing such protection for little-known and poorly appreciated wild plants and animals. This problem has not been resolved through either markets or public ownership.

Opposition to this privatization scheme may also stem from fear that one group or type of user may accumulate an overwhelming number of shares. Perhaps industry groups would pay more to buy and accumulate shares because the revenues returned for extractive uses (like timber harvest and mining) would be greater than the return on less extractive uses (such as conserving wildlife habitat and hiking). This is far from certain, especially since in many cases industry would want different tracts than the ones to which environmentalists or recreation groups would give high priority. Even if this happened, however, the rights gained from the auction are transferable. Preservation groups could negotiate with the new owners to preserve lands deemed valuable for critical wildlife habitat, recreation, or other non-extractive uses.

Today, many organizations successfully contract with private owners to obtain protection for wildlife, plant species, ecosystems, and landscapes. Stories abound from the Nature Conservancy, Audubon Society, Ducks Unlimited, the Rocky Mountain Elk Foundation, and many more about innovative ways to protect desired amenities, all funded by private-sector support. It is likely that more groups will form as our demand for improved environmental quality rises—and even more if there were the potential for ownership that such share certificates would create.

In spite of its shortcomings, such a privatization scheme would offer some benefits. To explore its merits, it would be useful to apply it in a small, experimental way. For example, a parcel of publicly owned land in a county could be disbursed to the citizens of that county through share certificates. This would provide invaluable lessons for public resource management. But so far few appear willing to take such a step.

Federal to State Ownership

With privatization unlikely, some have suggested that transferring federal lands to state ownership could improve management (O'Toole 1997; FLTF 2000), and in the past, many attempts have been made to hand off federal lands to more local control. In 1930, the Hoover administration offered land to the western states, but the offer was rejected (O'Toole 1997). The Sagebrush Rebellion of the late 1970s sparked resolutions from western congressmen requesting that the federal lands be turned over to state governments. In 1995 bills proposed in Congress would have transferred the administration of federal lands to the states in which they are located. Idaho has requested that federal lands within its boundaries be transferred to the state for administration (FLTF 2000).

The actual results of such a transfer would hinge on the rules under which the management occurs. States differ in the ways they manage their public lands, and agencies within each state differ as well. For example, state trust lands have a mandate to generate revenues, and this mandate is backed by interest groups such as school administrators, teachers, and parents. Many state park agencies, however, operate more like the federal government. Any revenues they earn go to the state treasury, and their budgets depend on legislative appropriations. As with federal land managers, different rules will provide different incentives.

Federal agencies expend significant resources to meet stringent federal regulations. If land is transferred to state governments, and all existing regulations and fees remain as they are now (such as abiding by NEPA and NFMA and returning revenues to the general treasury), state governments are expected to lose money except where the lands have significant mining operations. Robert Nelson estimated that the western states would lose $113 million under such a trade (Nelson 1994).

Changing the rules, however, could lead to different results. If all state agencies were required to generate revenues in excess of costs, they would be likely to charge market-based fees, whereas federal agencies generally do not. Refer back to chapter 2 and recall that while federal land agencies are paid a grazing fee of about $1.36 per animal-unit-month, state grazing fees generally range between $2 and $7.[1] In the case of timber, average state timber receipts exceed federal timber revenues by more than 60 percent per thousand board feet.[2] (Of course, differing resource quality and differing contract requirements also contribute to the discrepancy in revenues.) Although funding mechanisms vary across the states, the fact that states cannot legally develop and service deficits leads to greater cost control (see Souder and Fairfax 1996).

TRUST MANAGEMENT

Lands do not have to be transferred out of federal control to improve stewardship. There are many ways to change incentives. Some are worth replicating, others not. One of the most promising is trust management.

A trust is the legal assignment of certain powers to one or more persons, the trustee or trustees, who manage assets for the benefit of another individual or group (Anderson and Fretwell 1999, 5). Although many trusts provide private benefits only, such as holding money until a minor becomes an adult, a charitable trust can be created to use assets for the public benefit as designated by the donor. Land trusts, for example, are charitable trusts that have been formed to preserve habitat, open space, and forestlands.[3] As with other institutions, the incentives that influence trust management are defined by the underlying contracts.

Trusts provide financial accountability into the future, giving managers an incentive for long-term resource stewardship. State school trusts are the most widespread example of government trusts. Because they have a well-defined goal that can be measured and enforced, state trusts provide an excellent example of a public trust.

Many private conservation organizations are managed like trusts. These include the National Audubon Society, the Nature Conservancy, and land trusts, now numbered at more than 1,500 across the nation (Parker 2005).

In spite of their name, these are not always true trusts; they are sometimes legally defined as nonprofit organizations. But their composition draws on formal trust mechanisms in that they provide for the benefit of the public and are restricted by fiduciary responsibility.

Conservation institutions may set out to protect a specified species, habitat, or land type. Trout Unlimited (TU), for example, aims to protect and enhance trout and salmon fisheries. This goal benefits a particular segment of the public, whose donations make up over half of the organization's annual budget. Because the donors commit funds to the organization, they have an incentive to provide oversight to TU. If they perceive that TU is spending money frivolously, donations will decline.[4] Thus, an interested segment of the public monitors and enforces performance through its donations.

It is more difficult to enforce the terms of a charitable trust that is not publicly funded by its membership the way that Trout Unlimited is. Charitable trusts are expected to convey some benefit to society—and for that reason they do not pay taxes and donations to them are tax-deductible. The public is paying in part, through forgone tax revenues, for the benefits provided by the trust. Yet the public typically has little influence in enforcing the terms of the trust. A trust that fails to benefit the public is subject to action by the state attorney general. (The same would hold true for a trust overseen or funded by the government.) If the attorney general chooses not to act, little will be done.

In spite of this weakness, trusts offer increased accountability and a stronger link between the provider (the trust) and the beneficiary (the public) compared to traditional public management. Recognizing this potential, Congress has created two trusts that manage federal land, the Presidio Trust in San Francisco and the Valles Caldera in New Mexico.

The Presidio, a former military post overlooking San Francisco's Golden Gate Bridge, was transferred to the National Park Service and incorporated into the Golden Gate National Recreation Area when it was decommissioned in 1994. Congress created the Presidio Trust to manage the historical barracks, research installations, and other facilities in partnership with the National Park Service. Eventually, the trust is expected to be financially self-sufficient.

The legislation engendered a "wholly owned government corporation." It is based on trust ideas—managed by a seven-member board with the direct mission to "preserve and enhance the Presidio while making it financially self-sufficient by 2013." Unfortunately, there is no public oversight or enforcement mechanism. Congress must determine if the trust is operating properly, and it is to rely on accounts reported by the trust itself. If the board fails to achieve its fiduciary goal, the 1,480-acre Presidio and its 870 structures will be put up for sale or transferred out of federal ownership (PL 104–333).

The Valles Caldera National Preserve, formerly the Baca Ranch, is a similar experiment. Acquired by Congress in 2000, the preserve, too, is to be managed by a board of trustees, with the eventual goal of self-sufficiency. Its 89,000 acres of forest and high country meadows are nearly surrounded by the Santa Fe National Forest. As with the Presidio, a board manages the trust to protect and preserve it for the benefit of the public under congressional oversight.

Managing the trust is highly political; there are fourteen pages of federal instructions and six, sometimes competing, goals. Two of the goals are to manage the ranch as a preserve and to manage it as a working ranch. What has not been resolved is whether it is to be a working ranch with a protected reserve or a protected reserve with an isolated area for ranching. Trust managers have not been told which uses should take priority or how to determine priority status. Bill DeBuys, former chairman of the board, believes this is one of the vital problems of the trust that must be resolved through legislation.[5] With too many goals and no procedure to prioritize them, even trust management falls back to political decision-making. The land managed by the Valles Caldera Trust will revert to the Forest Service if the trust conditions for self-sufficiency are not met by 2017.

One benefit of trust management for public conservation is that the trustees have the ability to consider alternative resource values and the trade-offs between them. A trust has the potential ability to obtain revenues that can enhance land stewardship in ways other than simply relying on congressional appropriations. The decision not to drill for gas on a portion of trust land, for example, means the loss of potential revenues that could be used for conservation elsewhere.

The choices that some private land organizations have made on their own lands help demonstrate the benefits of considering other land uses as well as conservation:

- In 1981, the Baker Sanctuary, a refuge for sandhill cranes managed by the Michigan Audubon Society, initiated a lease for offsite, directional drilling of hydrocarbons. The marsh lake and swamp are protected by stringent lease conditions as defined by the society. Drilling was allowed only during non-nesting seasons, only one producing well was permitted, container restrictions were in place to prevent contamination, and any inadvertent damages were to be paid for by the drilling company. In return, the society received a royalty of 18.75 percent of proceeds that helped it continue its preservation mission (CEQ 1984, 372).

- The Rainey Preserve, a National Audubon Society sanctuary in Louisiana, allowed thirteen natural gas wells to be drilled onsite. The first well was drilled around 1950 and production continued until 1999 when it was no longer economical to produce. The wells generated about $25 million for the Audubon Society. Money was used to further conservation purposes.[6]
- The Nature Conservancy (TNC) has allowed for active land use that coincides with conservation purposes. TNC only purchases land that it considers critical for wildlife habitat or watershed protection, and it insists on having the financial resources to cover land-management costs. To provide the resources, the conservancy's Texas City Prairie Preserve, home of the endangered Atwater's prairie chicken, pumped out oil, generating $5.2 million for additional conservation. Members' perception that pumping is environmentally harmful has led TNC to discontinue the development of oil and gas on all their lands, however. It appears that TNC estimates the cost of losing members over this issue to be greater than the benefits.
- The Nature Conservancy's Pine Butte Guest Ranch supports itself as well as other conservation lands. This ranch abuts the eastern flank of the Bob Marshall Wilderness along the front, where the plains end and the mountains begin. The ranch is open to paying customers, and adjacent land is leased for livestock grazing and hay production. The preserve, bordering the ranch, protects an 18,000-acre wetland and wildlife corridor from the mountains to the plains (Fretwell 2000, 14).
- The Nature Conservancy has a growing number of landholdings that obtain revenues by offering recreation accommodations. The recently acquired Madden-Zapata Ranch in southern Colorado, part of the Great Sand Dunes, has extensive wetlands where sandhill cranes rest during their migration and where numerous other waterbirds make their home. Human visitors can take part in hiking, wildlife watching, mountain biking, and horseback riding. The ranch offers a restaurant and a naturalist workshop weekend.[7] TNC lodges are available for nightly accommodations at the Gray's Island Preserve in Virginia, Arizona's Hart Prairie Preserve, New Mexico's Bear Mountain Lodge, and the Blue Berry Mountain Inn in Pennsylvania, among others.[8] The Nags Head Woods Ecological Preserve in North Carolina provides day camps for children.
- The Nature Conservancy's success in linking conservation with economic productivity has inspired it to try out a different form of community-based conservation in the forests of southwestern Virginia. The Clinch Valley is 75 percent forested and home to animals and aquatic life that depend on the river system's clean water. To protect the health of the forest and watershed, the conservancy created what has become known as the forest bank. The forest bank works in partnership with private owners of land

and forests. Private owners make "deposits" in the bank in the form of the legal rights to grow, manage, and harvest trees on the land. The landowner retains ownership, but the bank assumes responsibility for all management costs and the risk of financial loss from forest depredation. The forest bank pays landowners an annual dividend based on the value of their forest deposit. To fund the payments, the forest bank harvests and sells timber on a sustainable basis, protecting critical wildlife habitat and water quality (Fretwell 2000, 15). By acquiring timber rights, TNC was able to achieve conservation goals that were too costly through land acquisition alone.

The experience of trusts, especially private ones but also those that manage state lands, shows that trust management offers flexibility that is similar to private ownership while retaining specified goals that the trustees must carry out with fiduciary responsibility. The steps that the federal government has taken in this direction are small and halting, but the example of other trusts suggests that this is a model that should be emulated.

STATE PARK SYSTEMS

State park systems provide close-to-home outdoor recreation opportunities and protect cultural, historical, natural, and recreational amenities. Covering nearly 13 million acres across the nation, state parks host more than 760 million visitors each year, more than all federal lands put together (NASPD 2000). Most state park agencies are funded in ways similar to their national counterpart, the National Park Service, rather than their state trust lands, but a growing number are changing the way they do business.

When fiscal budgets tighten, state agencies must be more creative in managing parklands. Although most budgets are still appropriated by the legislature, parks are relying more and more on user fees. In 2001, state parks generated more than one-third of their operating budgets, up from 23 percent in 1980, and nearly all of these funds are now returned to state park agencies rather than to the state's general treasury (Leal and Fretwell 1997; NASPD 2002). National park user receipts, on the other hand, cover a mere 9 percent of operations (NPS 2009). Seventeen state park systems obtained nearly half of their operating costs from user fees in fiscal year 2001. In fact, both New Hampshire and Vermont fund their entire operating budgets out of user fees (NASPD 2002).

A closer look shows that increased services, more and higher fees, and differential pricing have helped the agencies pick up the slack of funding shortfalls (see Leal and Fretwell 1997). Allowing revenues to be retained by the agency has encouraged innovative financing and created a direct link between park agencies and park users. As a result, visitors are getting more of the services they want and parks are getting the public support they need to stay in operation. These remain the exception, not the rule, however.

NATURAL RESOURCE AGENCIES

State wildlife agencies have the responsibility of managing existing fish and wildlife resources. State wildlife agencies are funded in part from license fees and taxes. The Pittman-Robertson Act of 1937, a key piece of legislation in support of state wildlife agencies, provides federal funds for the agencies from a tax on sporting goods and requires all hunting license revenues to be dedicated to state wildlife programs. Before the 1937 act, this money was often diverted to general state coffers.

Since the passage of the act, funding of state wildlife agencies has depended on demand for wildlife resources. Those who want better habitat for game pay for the management of it. The Dingell-Johnson Act of 1950 provided similar provisions for fishery resources. Fishing and hunting licenses made up 43 percent of all state agency funds in fiscal year 2000; another 21 percent was from dedicated federal taxes (WCFA 2001).[9] State general funds provided only 12 percent of wildlife agency budgets, though the amount from state appropriations is growing (WCFA 2001).

Just as various interests compete for the use of federal lands, wildlife interests are sometimes at odds. The traditional wildlife supporters are sportsmen who desire better habitat for game species. Their purchases of sporting equipment and licenses help fund the majority of agency budgets and as a group they have provided oversight ensuring state wildlife agencies are properly managing for game species. Currently, there is growing interest in nongame species and habitat, and sources of funding have expanded to include general state funds, state dedicated funding sources, tax check-off programs, lotteries, and wildlife license plates (Lueck 2000, 8). As important as it is to manage for both game and nongame species, as users become more disparate and funding less related to user desires, the ability of hunters and anglers to act as watchdogs is diminishing. Such oversight by user groups is part of the key to accountability. But for oversight to be effective the goals must be well defined and the overseers must have influence over decisions.

USER FEES: A MARKET TOOL

Whatever the form management takes (trust, traditional federal management, or state agencies), user fees are a valuable tool in improving visitor service and in helping maintain recreation and conservation areas. The key to improving the incentives through fees is for the revenues to be retained for onsite use.

Privately owned preserves such as Grandfather Mountain and Hawk Mountain Sanctuary provide spectacular bird watching, wildlife viewing, and hiking—for a fee. The Nature Conservancy and the Audubon Society take great care in protecting their lands to meet their conservation goals, relying on fees or private donations for managerial funds. Even timber companies such as International Paper and landowners who belong to the North Maine Woods manage their forests with attention to consumer demands for wildlife and amenity values, again with incentives and feedback provided by visitors to their properties. As we have seen, many federal lands do not charge fees; others charge much lower fees than other destinations such as theme parks and recreational sites; and in many cases whatever revenue they receive from fees is diverted to the federal treasury.

The current funding scheme for most federal land burdens taxpayers, distorts management decisions, and discourages private competition (because subsidized federal prices are lower than private owners can charge). Another result of today's management is that our public lands are overused. On an average summer day in Grand Canyon National Park, 6,000 cars show up at the South Rim to compete for 2,500 parking spots. In the Great Smoky Mountains, stop-and-go traffic extends an eleven-mile loop into four to six hours of travel time.[10] In Honolulu's Pearl Harbor, visitors may wait up to five hours to see a documentary film and take a boat to see the USS Arizona Memorial.[11] Rather than pay in cash for the desired services, visitors end up paying to a large extent in wasted time, while the quality of the trip decreases and environmental amenities are degraded by overuse.

The fees extended by the Federal Lands Recreation Enhancement Act, which are charged to the public for specific uses of public lands, are a step in the direction of better incentives. It has helped free managers from political pressures and encouraged them to respond to visitor demands and to protect resources. But the fee program has flaws, too.

First, visitors still contribute only a small portion of the overall budget for the park or forest unit. Much of the budget still depends on congressional appropriations. A second limitation is that the program rewards managers only for supplying recreation. Other values of parks and other public lands—such as protection of water quality for surrounding communities and in rivers and preserving nongame habitat—are not reflected in recreation fees. Yet these are important, too. If federal land managers better understood how visitors valued the resources—wilderness, water, habitat, and scenic views—they would be better able to provide for multiple uses. Unfortunately, in some of these cases it is difficult for consumers to pay for protecting wilderness or watersheds. As a result, markets alone may supply less than what consumers demand. Nevertheless, in spite of its flaws, the federal fee program is a step toward managerial accountability.

PUBLIC/PRIVATE PARTNERSHIPS

Some lands are managed through agreements or contracts between private groups and public land agencies. Arrangements of this type can be cost-effective and ensure good land stewardship when the private entity has a long-term commitment to the land. Agreements with local groups can help decentralize management decisions, providing greater influence by those directly affected by the land use. Such agreements take a variety of forms and vary widely from site to site and group to group.

Friends' Groups

One of the simplest forms of public/private partnerships is a friends' or trails' group that adopts a particular area or site. These nonprofit organizations encourage awareness, familiarity, and stewardship and build a base of supportive constituents. Some groups merely greet visitors and share information. Others provide volunteer services to restore trails, pick up trash, or paint buildings. Some raise funds to cover the costs of restoration and maintenance. Corporations may help underwrite major restoration projects. To support restoration of the Washington Monument, for example, which took place between 1996 and 2000, Target stores donated $2.5 million and helped raise another $4 million for the $10 million project (CNN.com 2000). Such groups assist with the upkeep of public land and may improve the link between the public and park managers.

Despite all of the good that such groups can do, the interests of the group may not be aligned with the interests of the public. For example, members may be interested in keeping a trail accessible only by foot, denying access to other types of uses that may be legitimate. A group's hard work and dedication could sway management decisions in ways that favor narrower goals.

Stewardship Contracts

Created as a demonstration project for the Forest Service, stewardship contracts are agreements between the Forest Service, a local community, and a hired contractor[12] to conduct a specific project, one that will restore a landscape in a way that is consistent with community goals. These innovative contracts can help overcome the paralysis that plagues forest management.

They differ from traditional contracts for timber sales or particular services on forestland. First, a variety of services—rather than just harvesting timber—may be performed. These can include cutting timber, clearing brush, restoring roads, or improving campsites. Typically, the contractor removes and sells timber, generating funds that help pay for the rest of the work. Alternatively, the agency may hire two contractors; one that pays the agency for commercially valuable timber products that it removes, and one that is paid with those same timber revenues to complete the remaining service work desired.

Stewardship contracts originated as part of an effort to expedite restoration and maintenance work on national forests. They fill a void for the Forest Service. Under current regulations, service contracts are available for services such as brush clearing, where there is little or no commercial value to the material to be removed.[13] But legislated funds must be available to pay for the service. Timber sale contracts are available when the commercial value of the timber exceeds the direct cost of its removal, and private companies pay the government for the opportunity to harvest the timber. Stewardship contracts fall in between, allowing the value of materials removed to be used in payment for the contracted restoration work. In 1999, the Forest Service was authorized to initiate twenty-eight pilot stewardship contracts.

Stewardship contracts involve a broad-based public collaboration process that identifies the goal. For example, a goal may be a thinned forest leaving a specific number of large trees per acre and removing all bushy undergrowth. Usually referred to as the prescription, this final product is defined by all of the interested parties, and a multiyear contract is awarded to the winning bidder. The bids are evaluated in several ways. In addition to price, individual or firm historical performance, the quality of past work, and experience in the field may help determine the winning bid.

Stewardship projects emphasize collaboration. From the development of project criteria through implementation, input from all participating partners is considered. Local, regional, and national assessment teams work together to collect and analyze data for project evaluation.

Although these contracts are a step in the right direction, their focus on collaboration makes them time-consuming and costly. It can take years of hard work for a collaborative group to reach consensus on forest treatment. And even with stewardship projects, the Forest Service still has an incentive to emphasize timber removal, because the revenues from the contracts can fund other services on the site. Stewardship contracts decentralize decision-making, but the emphasis on timber harvest has not changed.

NATURE AND RECREATIONAL LEASES

Additional ideas that have yet to be tested could improve management of the federal estate. Perhaps the most promising would be to allow private owners and nonprofit groups to lease federal land. These would fill a critical need that even the Federal Demonstration Program does not address. Fees lead to better service and protection of resources, but most fees are for recreation. They do not influence the management to provide for alternative resource uses such as research, wildlife habitat protection, and water quality.

To move beyond this omission, private parties or nonprofit groups could bid in a competitive auction for the right to use the resources. Such leases would give these groups direct control over specific tracts of land. Leases prepared by the land managers would specify potential use of the land as well as any prohibited uses. For example, an area forested with old-growth trees might be leased to a group interested in habitat protection for wildlife, and timber harvesting would not be allowed. In an area of second growth, however, the land might be leased for commercial timber harvest or even the collection of other forest products. Nature leasing would be a way for land managers to mitigate multiple-use conflicts while reducing the costs of management and earning additional revenue.

The public agency that issues the lease would make the initial decisions about the leases, unless a private, local group was given this responsibility. The process will remain somewhat political. For example, it would decide what lease options were available on various parcels; it would set stewardship goals and would periodically evaluate land conditions. It would specify the exact area covered by the lease as well as the length of the lease. The leases could be long-term, encompassing at least one timber rotation, or short-term, such as five years with an annual assessment that would continue to add an additional year given satisfactory management. Leases could follow the lead of Canadian evergreen timber leases that provide for renewable timber harvest leases (see Berry 2006). In some cases bonding would be beneficial to ensure stewardship goals are met or to cover any external harm to neighboring lands.

The necessary oversight, as discussed above, could be done by the agency but perhaps more appropriately by the local citizens who will be most affected. Those who live near the land will benefit most from good stewardship through enhanced recreation values, water quality, or timber revenues. Local citizens will also bear the greatest burden of poor management whether it is excessive timber harvest that damages the water quality and recreation or too little active management resulting in overly dense forests, reduced water yield, and greater risk of a wildfire disaster.

For many federal lands having little or no value for production of commodities, environmental leasing would be a low-cost way to resolve the conflict over uncontrolled recreation. For example, groups or individuals could lease land for habitat protection or exclusive hunting and fishing privileges. The leaseholder could choose to set off an area as a sanctuary for wildlife, not allowing any consumptive activities to take place. Or the leaseholder could allow hunting and fishing on a fee basis. It would also be possible for the leaseholder to sublease the land for an alternative, but nonconflicting use, to maximize revenues. For example, it might be possible to hold a lease for exclusive fishing rights, but sublet the right for scientific research to a university. Similarly, the Forest Service or Bureau of Land Management could offer a lease with an option to bid on all or some of the potential land uses. The revenues from the leases would then flow back to the respective federal land agency to help pay for the management of the leases.

Nature groups such as the Rocky Mountain Elk Foundation, the Nature Conservancy, Ducks Unlimited, and Trout Unlimited could use recreational leases as a way to finance their primary goal of bringing more acreage under protection for fish and wildlife purposes. Just as TNC does on many of its lands, visitors could pay a fee. Various interpretive programs could be provided and friends' groups could help with restoration and maintenance. Such leases would allow groups to reduce crowding on federal lands where overuse is causing deterioration of environmental and recreational quality.

In areas that have the potential for profitable commodity production as well as significant environmental values such as streams for salmon spawning, environmental leasing can provide options to the highly polarized political process often used today. If a nonprofit group is interested in maintaining the environmental values of the area, for example, it can lease the land and assume managerial responsibility for deciding if, where, how, and how much production takes place. Like Audubon's Rainey Preserve, drilling for oil or gas could be allowed but only under conditions dictated by the group's conservation objectives. As opposed to the all-or-nothing outcomes of the political process, nature leasing provides an incentive to the leaseholder to weigh the benefits that could come from carefully planned and supervised commodity production.

States have already begun to experiment with such leasing and similar market transactions that both protect state lands and raise revenue for public coffers. A number of environmental groups have taken the states up on their market offers and put cash on the counter for the right to participate in public land management decisions.

- Abandoning court battles and protests, a coalition of environmental groups bought the right not to cut timber on 25,000 acres of Loomis State Forest in north-central Washington. The land is the only remaining roadless area in the two-million-acre Loomis State Forest. One thing that makes the Loomis deal significant is the size of the payment—$13.1 million. The deal marks the first time that private funds have been used to change how a government forest is managed.

- The state of Montana has permitted timber sales that have a nonharvest option. In 1998, the state proposed a timber sale, known as the Two Crow sale. The local community preferred to see the trees standing. It paid for a provision that would leave trees standing on a portion of the land for ten years.[14]
- Montana's Department of Natural Resources and Conservation is now granting conservation leases, similar to the nature leases discussed above. Traditional state land leases required consumptive uses such as grazing or timber harvest. More recently, the stipulations of some leases have changed to allow the land to be managed solely for wildlife. The first conservation lease on Montana school trust lands, granted to the Nature Conservancy, allowed the Conservancy to manage the land mostly for wildlife, recreation, and research. It will generate about $2,500 per year more than a general grazing lease would have.[15]
- In Colorado, conservation leases earn the state school trust $340,000 per year. One leaseholder, who leases Chico Basin Ranch from the state, attracts artists to the ranch because of the attractiveness of the area. They pay a portion of the proceeds from the sale of their artwork to the leaseholder to help support the ranch and pay for the lease.
- Wyoming has engaged in a conservation easement that restricts development on state-owned properties near Jackson Hole. The deal, made with a private land trust, generated $1.2 million for the school trust.
- Some states are experimenting with allowing bids on traditional grazing lands for nongrazing uses. The first nongrazing lease on state trust rangeland was awarded in 1996 in New Mexico. The Forest Guardians, an environmental group, outbid a rancher for a 644-acre riparian area. The state trust now receives not only greater revenues from the new lessee, but willows and other cover have been planted along damaged stream banks. New Mexico now has several range land leases for nongrazing use, although the majority remain traditional grazing leases. The state also allows lessees to sublet the land for alternative uses with the permission of the state land commissioner.
- Arizona, like New Mexico, allows bidding for alternative uses on traditional grazing allotments.
- Montana has allowed alternative bidding on some traditional state grazing lands. In 1999, a grazing lease with the potential to generate $267,600 over a twenty-year period came up for renewal. In an effort to maximize

revenues, the state solicited bids for grazing as well as other uses such as outfitting, sites for cabins, and commercial timber harvest (Fretwell 2000, 12). By selling various resource uses on the same land, the 12,000-acre allotment will now generate $1.5 million over twenty years. Although these leases still provide mostly grazing, the lessees could choose to bid on additional rights for each lease allotment.[16] For example, on one unit the lessee did not purchase the timber rights. As a result, the right to harvest timber was retained by the department, but the lessee could have purchased the right, restricting commercial harvest over the twenty-year lease. Other states are providing leases on public lands for recreational opportunities.

- In Mississippi, recreational leases on state trust lands generate an average $24 per acre.
- Minnesota recreation leases produce revenues from state trust lands in excess of their costs.
- Even remote state lands in Utah's desert areas can attract paying users. The Utah State School Trust Agency has leased one plot of desert land to the Mission from Mars Society for scientific research and study.

The state school trusts are learning they can provide for conservation, wildlife, and environmental amenities while meeting their fiscal mandates. As demand and interest rise, these agencies are turning to nontraditional land-use leases such as recreation, nature, and conservation leases to meet their financial obligations. Federal land agencies also could serve the public, achieve better stewardship, and improve cost-effectiveness by allowing alternative land-use leases.

Although nature leasing, to the extent it occurs now, is paid for by nonprofit organizations such as the Nature Conservancy and Forest Guardians, the financing of nature leases could be provided through citizen shares as suggested by Anderson, Smith, and Simmons (1999) in their proposal to privatize public lands. Every citizen would receive a certificate of ownership, which could be retained, donated, or sold to another individual or group. The certificates could be used as currency in public land leasing. In this case land ownership would not be auctioned, only the right to use the land, a public umbrella organization would provide oversight and maintain land ownership.

As a first step, federal land agencies would identify all current uses of their lands as well as the land's ecological capacity for alternative uses. Then rights for use could be leased through auction with the limitation that the use must be within the ecological constraints of the land. Individuals or groups who purchased the rights could choose either to use these rights actively or to retire them, but the rights would remain transferable. That is, a hiking group might choose to purchase the rights to off-road vehicle use with the intention of retiring them. However, if an off-road vehicle group then made an acceptable offer to buy those rights from the hiking group, the off-roaders would be able to negotiate to reestablish those use rights on the land if it stayed within the previously defined ecological capacity of the land.

Use would be monitored and some resources managed by a public agency, trust, or board. The board could charge user fees to cover management expenses, so long as they were announced prior to the auction. The budget of the board would be constrained by fee receipts, donations, and auction revenue; no additional public revenues would be available to support the board (see Lipford et al. 2002).

The federal government is slowly trying out land-management approaches that offer more flexibility and mimic market institutions in at least some respects. Testing these ideas on pilot sites and evaluating the outcome can help provide insight for new management approaches. Much more should be done.

CONCLUSION: TRIAL REFORMS TO GET THE INCENTIVE RIGHT

This book has examined the difficulties faced when federal bureaucracies are set up to manage landscapes. A variety of solutions have been proposed to help improve the stewardship of the federally owned lands. While divestiture of federal lands requires a leap of faith that most Americans are not ready to take, the same incentives that motivate private property owners also can be used to motivate public land managers.

Some progress has been made; certainly the Federal Demonstration Program is improving the incentives for recreation managers. By reestablishing the link between land managers and land users through fees that remain onsite, the manager once again becomes accountable to the user and not to politicians. Stewardship contracts are proving useful tools for federal forest management, allowing private contractors to use the timber they remove to pay for the restoration services they perform. Public-private partnerships hold some promise, although oversight is essential to ensure that the self-interest of the private partner is in the best interest of the public as well.

Much more must be done to enhance the stewardship of our public lands. Nature and recreational leases could help lead to long-term husbandry of the land. In taking these steps, it would be worthwhile to establish more experimental sites on public lands. Those in charge of the sites should have the flexibility to pursue innovative options that can help lead the way to new management structures.

Environmental protection should be allowed to compete with traditional land uses. As long as managers receive revenues from only the more extractive uses—timber, grazing, minerals, and even recreation—they will have an incentive to emphasize these uses over others. But markets for conservation and environmental amenities exist, as shown by the rising number of land and conservation trusts. At the same time, current resource uses must be weighed against future value. It is the long-term outlook that constrains use within its ecological capacity. In the case of state trust lands, the requirement for perpetual income generation enhances the long-term view for resource conservation.

In sum, alternative mechanisms must be introduced into public land management to improve the stewardship of federal lands, enhance accountability, and control costs. Under the current system land use is allocated by politics. By providing federal land managers with new incentives and reducing the ties to congressional funding, it may be possible to reshape federal land management to benefit the public by introducing more desired uses without compromising environmental integrity.

NOTES

1. In this document the following data sources shall be referred to as BLM: BLM expenditure and receipt data for the period 1998 to 2001 are from *Budget Justifications* (BLM 1998–2003); *Public Land Statistics* (BLM 1998–2001); BLM FOIA request of November 29, 2001; telephone and written communication with Lori Castaneda, BLM accountant, Denver; onshore minerals costs and receipts are from Minerals Management Service, available at www.mrm.mms.gov/stats/pdfdocs/coll_lc.pdf; and telephone and written communication with James Stockbridge, Budget Officer, Minerals, Revenue Management, Mineral Management Service, Denver.

The following data sources shall be hereinafter referred to as FSD: Forest Service expenditure and receipt data for the 1998 to 2001 period are from *1999 Budget Explanatory Notes* (FS 1999); *Budget Justifications* (FS 2000–2002); written communication with William Helin, Program & Budget Analysis Staff, Forest Service, Washington, D.C.; and written communication with Richard Thornburgh, Program & Budget Analysis Staff, Forest Service, Washington, D.C.

The following data sources shall be hereinafter referred to as NPSD: National Park Service expenditure and receipt data are from *Budget Request* (NPS 1999–2002); *Recreational Fee Demonstration Program Report to Congress* (USDI & USDA 2001).

2. See BLM and FSD above.

3. Some organizations described here are not legal trusts; rather, they are nonprofits. For practical purposes here, however, they act like trusts in that they manage assets for the benefit of others. See Fairfax and Guenzler 2001 for a definitive explanation.

4. On the other hand, if the interested public sees trout habitat as plentiful and sufficient they may feel supporting TU for increased habitat is unwarranted. This also brings to surface the free-rider problem; if it is assumed that others will pay for the habitat enhancements, the free rider will not put forth addition resources.

5. Personal communication with Bill DeBuys, September 16, 2005.

6. Written communication from Michael Crago, Orleans Audubon Society, January 14, 2001.

7. 2003 Medan-Zapata Naturalist Ranch Workshops, available at http://nature .org/wherewework/northamerica/states/colorado/files/mzworkshops03.pdf.

8. http://nature.org/magazine/jan_2001/mag_foorprints.html.

9. The federal tax receipts appropriated as designated by the Pittman-Robertson Act (16 USC 668–669) for guns and ammunition and the Dingell-Johnson Act of 1950 for fishing equipment allocate funds based on state land area, state population, and state hunter numbers. The Dingell-Johnson Act was amended in 1984 by the Wallop-Breaux Act (16 USC 777), adding boating tax revenues.

10. NPCA, "Across the Nation," available at http://www.npca.org/across_the_ nation/visitor_experience/tea21.asp.

11. www.nps.gov/usar/pphtml/planyourvisit.html. Cited December 28, 2005.

12. The Forest Service's Stewardship Contracting Pilot Program was authorized by Congress in Section 347 of the FY 1999 Omnibus Appropriations Act (P.L. 05-277).

13. Service contracts allow only negatively valued material or material valued at less than $10,000 to be removed and sold by the contractor (Forest Service Handbook 2409).

14. Beverly O'Brien, DNRC, Kalispell, personal communication, May 21, 2002.

15. Mark Ahner, Montana DNRC, written and personal communication, February 20, 2002.

16. Written communication from Mark Ahner, Area manager, Central Land Office, MDNRC, March 22, 1999.

Bibliography

Aggarwal, Raj, and Joel T. Harper. 2000. Equity Valuation in the Czech Voucher Privatization Auctions. *Financial Management,* Winter. Online: http://www.findarticles .com/p/articles/mi_m4130/is_4_29/ai_69414439 (cited April 20, 2006).

Ament, Robert. 1997. *Fire Policy for the Northern Rocky Mountains (U.S.A).* Green Paper 12. Bozeman, MT: American Wildlands.

Americans for Our Heritage and Recreation. 2000. *The Land and Water Conservation Fund: A Guide to 35 Years of Success.* Washington, D.C. Online: www.hrinfo .org/AHR_report.pdf (cited February 29, 2000).

———. 1991. *Free Market Environmentalism.* Boulder, CO: Westview Press.

Anderson, Terry L., and Donald R. Leal. 1991. *Free Market Environmentalism.* Boulder, CO: Westview Press.

———. 1997. *Enviro-Capitalists: Doing Good While Doing Well.* Lanham, MD: Rowman & Littlefield.

———. 2001. *Free Market Environmentalism: Revised Edition.* New York, NY: Palgrave.

Anderson, Terry L., and Holly Lippke Fretwell. 1999. A Trust for the Grand Staircase-Escalante. *PERC Policy Series* PS-16. Bozeman, MT: PERC, September.

Anderson, Terry L., and Peter J. Hill. 2004. *The Not So Wild, Wild West.* Stanford, CA: Stanford University Press.

Anderson, Terry L., Vernon L. Smith, and Emily Simmons. 1999. How and Why to Privatize Federal Lands. *CATO Policy Analysis* No. 363. Washington, D.C.: CATO Institute, November.

Arizona State Land Department. 1998–2001. *Annual Report.* Phoenix.

Arno, Stephen F., and Steven Allison-Bunnell. 2002. *Flames in Our Forest: Disaster or Renewal?* Washington, D.C.: Island Press.

Audubon Advisory. New Administration, New Congress, New Challenges. 2001. January 19. Online: http://www.audubon.org/campaign/aa/archives/aa0011901. html (cited April 3, 2003).

Bahls, Jane Easter. 1990. Forest Fun: Fee or Free? *American Forests* 96(1–2): 28–33.

Baldwin, L. H., R. C. Marshall, and J. F. Richard. 1997. Bidder Collusion at Forest Service Timber Sales. *Journal of Political Economy* 105: 657–699.

Ballard, Ernesta. 2002. Why the Forest Service Misunderstands its Stewardship Role. Presented at Ketchikan, Alaska. Tongass National Forest: The Next 100 Years. August 20.

Bean, Michael. 1994. Speech at the U.S. Fish and Wildlife Service's Office of Training and Education Seminar Series, "Ecosystem Approaches to Fish and Wildlife Conservation: 'Rediscovering the Land Ethic'." November 3. Marymount University, Arlington, VA.

Beard, Charles A., and Mary R. Beard. 1960. *New Basic History of the United States.* New York, NY: Doubleday & Co.

Berry, Alison. 2006. *Branching Out: Case Studies in Canadian Forest Management.* Bozeman, MT: Property and Environment Research Center.

Bick, Steven, and Harry L. Haney Jr. 1999. *Conservation Easements.* Chicago, IL: American Farm Bureau.

Bonnicksen, Thomas M. 2000. *America's Ancient Forests.* Hoboken, NJ: John Wiley & Sons.

———. 2001. Written statement for the legislative hearing on H.R. 2119 National Historic Forests Act of 2001, United States House of Representatives. Washington, D.C. June 19.

Bosch, J. M., and J. D. Hewlett. 1982. A Review of Catchment Experiments to Determine the Effect of Vegetation Changes on Water Yield and Evapotranspiration. *Journal of Hydrology* 55: 2–23.

Bureau of the Census. 2000. *Statistical Abstract of the United States.* Washington, D.C.: Government Printing Office.

Bureau of Land Management (BLM). 1998–2003. *Budget Justifications.* Washington, D.C.: Department of the Interior.

———. 1998–2001. *Public Land Statistics.* Washington, D.C.: Department of the Interior.

Burk, Dale A. 1970. *The Clearcut Crisis: Controversy in the Bitterroot.* Great Falls, MT: Jursnick Printing.

Cameron, Jenks. 1928. *The Development of Governmental Forest Control in the United States.* Baltimore, MD: John Hopkins University Press.

Clark, Lance R., and R. Neil Sampson. 1995. *Forest Ecosystem Health in the Inland West: A Science Policy Reader.* Washington, D.C.: American Forests, Forest Policy Center.

Clawson, Marion. 1983. *The Federal Lands Revisited.* Resources for the Future. Washington, D.C.

CNN.com. 2000. *Washington Monument Restoration Celebrated.* July 3. Online: http://www.cnn.com/2000/US/07/03/monument.02/ (cited April 12, 2004).

Colorado State Board of Land Commissioners. Various years. *Annual Report.* Denver.

The Columbia Basin Bulletin (CBB). 2008. *USFWS Pacific Region States Get $12.3 Million in ESA Grants.* March 21. Bend, Oregon.

Committee on Agriculture. 1997. *Hearing on Forest Ecosystem Health in the United States.* Joint with Committee on Resources. Washington, D.C., April 9. Online:

http://commdocs.house.gov/committees/ag/hagforest.000/hagforest_0.htm (cited June 1, 2007).

Congressional Budget Office. 1999. *Maintaining Budgetary Discipline: Spending and Revenue Options.* Washington, D.C. CRS Report for Congress, Order code Rl33531. Carol Hardy Vincent. Washington, D.C., July 10.

Conservation Biology Institute and World Wildlife Fund USA. 1999. *Protected Areas Database.* November. Corvallis, OR.

Consortium for Research on Renewable Industrial Materials (CORRIM). 2001. CORRIM: A Report of Progress and a Glimpse of the Future. *Forest Products Journal* 51(10): 10–22.

Cornell, Stephen, and Joseph P. Kalt. 1992. Culture and Institutions as Public Goods. In *Property Rights and Indian Economies*, ed. Terry L. Anderson. Lanham, MD: Rowman & Littlefield, 215–52.

Council on Environmental Quality (CEQ). 1984. *The Fifteenth Annual Report of the Council of Environmental Quality Together with the President's Message to Congress.* Washington, D.C.: US GPO.

CRS Report for Congress. 2006. Land and Water Conservation Fund: Overview, Funding History, and Current Issues. Received through the CRS Web Order Code RL33531. July 10.

Davis, Kent. 1999. *Privatization in the Balance.* Michigan Privatization Report MPR1999-04. Online: www.mackinac.org/article.asp?ID=2558 (cited April 17, 2000).

Devlin, Sherry. 2004. Group Simmers Over Wildfire Recovery Plan. *The Missoulian*, February 7. Online: http://www.montanaforum.com/rednews/2004/02/07/build/forests/recovery.php?nnn=2 (cited April 8, 2004).

Discovery News Brief. 1999. December 31.

Donaldson, Thomas. 1970. *The Public Domain: Its History With Statistics.* New York: Johnson Reprint Corp.

Donato, D. C., J. B. Fontaine, J. L. Campbell, W. D. Robinson, J. B. Kauffman, and B. E. Law. 2006. Post-Wildfire Logging Hinders Regeneration and Increases Fire Risk. *Science* 311: 352 (January 20).

Eggertsson, Thráinn. 1990. *Economic Behavior and Institutions.* Cambridge, MA: Cambridge University Press.

Evergreen Magazine. 1994–1995. A Season of Fire. Winter: 48–57.

Fairfax, Sally K., and Darla Guenzler. 2001. *Conservation Trusts.* Lawrence, KS: University Press of Kansas.

Federal Land Task Force Working Group (FLTF). 2000. *Breaking the Gridlock: Federal Land Pilot Projects in Idaho.* A Report to the Idaho State Board of Land Commissioners. Boise, ID: FLTF, December.

Federal Parks & Recreation. 1999. Change Won't Come Easily to Big Conservation Bill. December 3.

Fedkiw, John. 1996. *Managing Multiple Uses on National Forests, 1905–1995.* Washington, D.C.: USDA, Forest Service.

Fish and Wildlife Service (FWS). 2006. *Fish and Wildlife Service Fiscal Year 2007 Budget Justifications.* Washington, D.C.: USDI. Online: http://www.fws.gov/budget/2007/FY%202007%20GB/toc.html (cited May 18, 2006).

Forest Guardians. 2000. *Eco-Defense & Zero-Cut Logging*. Online: http://www
.fguardians.org/ecodef.html (cited August 23, 2000).

Forest Service (FS). 1994. *Record of Decision for Amendments to Forest Service and Bureau of Land Management Planning Documents within the Range of the Northern Spotted Owl*. Washington, D.C.: USDA and USDI, Bureau of Land Management, April 13.

———. 1998a. *FY 1998 Budget Explanatory Notes for the Committee on Appropriations*. Washington, D.C.: U.S. Department of Agriculture.

———. 1998b. *USDA Forest Service Natural Resource Agenda Website: Forest Roads*. October 14. Online: http://www.fs.fed.us/news/agenda/roads.html (cited March 13, 2001).

———. 1998c. *Report of the Forest Service*. Washington, D.C.: U.S. Department of Agriculture.

———. 1998d. *Forest Management Program Annual Report*. Washington, D.C.: U.S. Department of Agriculture.

———. 1999. *Report of the Forest Service Fiscal Year 1998*. Washington, D.C.: USDA. Online: http://www.fs.fed. us/pl/pdb/98report/ (cited March 13, 2001).

———. 2000a. *Evaluating the Effectiveness of Postfire Rehabilitation Treatments*. General Technical Report RMRS-GTR-63. Fort Collins, CO: Rocky Mountain Research Station.

———. 2000b. *Report of the Forest Service 2001*. Washington, D.C.: USDA. Online: http://www.fs.fed.us/publications/2001/2001_Report_of_FS.pdf (cited May 29, 2003).

———. 2000c. *Forest Service Roadless Area Conservation: Draft Environmental Impact Statement*. Washington, D.C.: USDA, Forest Service.

———. 2000d. *Water and the Forest Service*. Washington, D.C.: USDA.

———. 2000e. *Rangeland Resource Trends in the United States*. RMRS-GTR-68. Washington, D.C.: USDA.

———. 2000–2002. *Budget Justifications*. Washington, D.C.: U.S. Department of Agriculture.

———. 2001. *Land Areas of the National Forest System*. FS-383. Washington, D.C.: USDA.

———. 2002. *The Process Predicament: How Statutory, Regulatory, and Administrative Factors Affect National Forest Management*. Washington, D.C.: USDA.

Foresta, R.A. 1984. *America's National Parks and Their Keepers*. Washington, D.C.: Resources for the Future.

Forsgren, Harv. 2000. Recreation: It's a Tough Climb. *Western Forester,* September/October.

Fretwell, Holly Lippke. 1998. The Price We Pay. *Public Lands Report I*. Bozeman, MT: PERC, August.

———. 1999a. Forests: Do We Get What We Pay For? *Public Lands Report II*. Bozeman, MT: PERC, July.

———. 1999b. Paying to Play: The Fee Demonstration Program. *PERC Policy Series* PS-17. Bozeman, MT: PERC.

———. 2000. Federal Estate: Is Bigger Better? *Public Lands Report III*. Bozeman, MT: PERC.

———. 2001. Is No Use Good Use? *Public Lands Report IV.* Bozeman, MT: PERC.

Gates, Paul W. 1984. The Federal Lands: Why We Retained Them. In *Rethinking the Federal Lands,* ed. Sterling Brubaker. Washington, D.C.: Resources for the Future.

General Accounting Office (GAO). 1982. *Increasing Entrance Fees – National Park Service.* Washington, D.C.

———. 1988. *Rangeland Management: More Emphasis Needed on Declining and Overstocked Grazing Allotments.* GAO/RCED-88-80. Washington, D.C.

———. 1995. *National Parks: Difficult Choices Need to be Made about the Future of the Parks.* GAO/RCED-95-238. Washington, D.C., August.

———. 1996. *Land Ownership: Information on the Acreage, Management, and Use of Federal and Other Lands.* GAO/RCED-96-40. Washington, D.C.

———. 1998a. *Forest Service: Lack of Performance and Financial Accountability has Resulted in Inefficiency and Waste.* GAO/T-RCED/ALMD-98-135. Washington, D.C., November.

———. 1998b. *Forest Service: Status of Progress Toward Financial Accountability.* GAO/AIMD-98-84. Washington, D.C., November.

———. 1998c. *Forest Service: Distribution of Timber Sales Receipts, Fiscal Years 1995 through 1997.* GAO/RCED-99-24. Washington, D.C., November.

———. 2000a. *Reducing Wildfire Threats: Funds Should Be Targeted to the Highest Risk Areas.* GAO/T-RCED-00-296. Washington, D.C.

———. 2000b. *Forest Service Roadless Areas: Potential Impact of Proposed Regulations on Ecological Sustainability.* GA047. Washington, D.C., November.

———. 2000c. *Proposed Regulations Adequately Address Some, but Not All, Key Elements of Forest Planning.* GA0/RCED-00-256. Washington, D.C., September.

———. 2002a. *Wildland Fire Management: Reducing the Threat of Wildland Fires Requires Sustained and Coordinated Effort.* Washington, D.C.

———. 2002b. *National Park Service: Status of Efforts to Develop Better Deferred Maintenance Data.* Washington, D.C., April 12. Online: http://www.gao.gov/new .items/d02568r.pdf. (cited August 19, 2004).

———. 2003a. *Forest Service: Information on Decisions Involving Fuels Reduction Activities.* Washington, D.C., May 14.

———. 2003b. *National Park Service: Status of Agency Efforts to Address its Maintenance Backlog.* GAO-03-992T. Washington, D.C., July 8.

———. 2003c. *Wildland Fire Management.* GAO-03-805. Washington, D.C., August.

Glickman, Dan. 1997. *Hearing on the Use of Fire as a Management Tool and its Risks and Benefits for Forest Health and Air Quality.* Statement of the Secretary, USDA, before the Committee on Resources, House of Representatives. Washington, D.C., September 30.

Grigg, Norman. 2000. Lock 'em Up, Burn 'em Down. *The New American.* September 25.

Hayward, Steven. 2000. The Suburbanization of America: In *A Guide to Smart Growth,* ed. Jane S. Shaw and Ronald D. Utt. Washington D.C.: The Heritage Foundation and Bozeman, MT: PERC.

Hess, Karl, Jr. 1993. *Rocky Times in Rocky Mountain National Park.* Niwot: University Press of Colorado.

Hessen, Robert. 1993. Corporations. In *The Fortune Encyclopedia of Economics*, ed. David E. Henderson. New York, NY: Warner Books.

Idaho Department of Health and Welfare (IDHW). 1997. *Forest Practices Water Quality Audit*. Boise, ID: Division of Environmental Quality, February.

Idaho Department of Lands. Various years. *Annual Report*. Boise.

Jackson, David H. 1987. Why Stumpage Prices Differ Between Ownerships: A Statistical Examination of State and Forest Service Sales in Montana. *Forest Ecology and Management* 18: 219–236.

Janofsky, Michael. 1999. The Crisis in the Parks: National Parks, Strained by Record Crowds, Face a Crisis. *New York Times*. July 25.

Jenson, Michael C., and William H. Meckling. 1976. Theory of the Firm: Managerial Behavior, Agency Costs, and Ownership Structure. *Journal of Financial Economics* 3(4): 305–360.

Kay, Charles E. 1997. Yellowstone: Ecological Malpractice. *PERC Reports*. Special Issue. Bozeman, MT: Political Economy Research Center, June.

Keegan, Charles E. III, Daniel P. Wichman, et al. 1996. Timber management costs: a comparison among major landowners in Idaho and Montana. *Montana Business Quarterly*, 34(2): 9–14.

Krutilla, John V. 1967. Conservation Reconsidered. *The American Review* 57(4): 777–786.

Kumlien, Kris. 2002. How the Milesnicks Found Markets. *PERC Reports*. Bozeman, MT: PERC, March.

Land Trust Alliance (LTA). 1998. *National Directory of Conservation Land Trusts*. Washington, D.C.

———. 2000. *2000 National Directory of Conservation Land Trusts*. Washington, D.C. Online: www.lta.org/aboutlta/census.shtml (cited March 11, 2003).

Langston, Nancy. 1995. *Forest Dreams/Forest Nightmares: The Paradox of Old Growth in the Inland West*. Seattle, WA: University of Washington Press.

Leal, Donald R. 1995. Turning a Profit on Public Forests. *PERC Policy Series* PS-4. Bozeman, MT: PERC.

Leal, Donald R., and Holly Lippke Fretwell. 1997. Back to the Future to Save Our Parks. *PERC Policy Series* PS-10. Bozeman, MT: PERC, June.

Libecap, Gary D., and Ronald N. Johnson. 1979. Property Rights, Nineteenth-Century Federal Timber Policy, and the Conservation Movement. *The Journal of Economic History* 39(1): 129–142.

Lindsay, Cotton M. 1976. A Theory of Government Enterprise. *Journal of Political Economy*. 84(October): 1061–1077.

Lipford, Jody, Jerry Slice, and Bruce Yandle. 2002. *South Carolina's Jocassee Gorges—Private Vice or Public Virtue*. PERC Research Study RS 02-2. Bozeman, MT. Online: http://www.perc.org/perc.php?subsection=9&id=209 (cited June 12, 2006).

Lueck, Dean. 1995. The Economic Organization of Wildlife Institutions. In *Wildlife in the Marketplace*, ed. Terry L. Anderson, and Peter J. Hill. Lanham, MD: Rowman & Littlefield.

——. 2000. *An Economic Guide to State Wildlife Management.* PERC Research Study RS 00-2. Bozeman, MT. Online: http://www.perc.org/perc.php?subsection=9&id=211 (cited June 12, 2006).

MacCleery, Douglas W. 1996. *American Forests: A History of Resiliency and Recovery.* Durham, NC: Forest History Society.

——. 1999. *The U.S. Experience in Managing Federal Forest Lands: Are There Some Lessons for Canada?* Paper prepared for Sylvicon 2000, Fredericton, New Brunswick, February 23–24, 2000.

Mackintosh, Barry. 1983. *Visitor Fees in the National Park System: A Legislative and Administrative History.* Washington, D.C.: National Park Service.

——. 1991. *The National Parks.* Harpers Ferry, WV: Harpers Ferry Center.

——. 1999. *The National Park Service: A Brief History.* Online: http://www.cr.nps.gov/history/hisnps/NPSHistory/npshisto.htm (cited May 23, 2006).

Mather, Stephen. 1916. *Progress in the Development of the National Parks.* Washington, D.C.: USDI.

Mathews, Mark. 1997. Wet Summer a Bust for Firefighters. *High Country News* 29 (17), September 15.

McCabe, Richard E. 1999. *Outdoor News Bulletin.* Washington, D.C.: Wildlife Management Institute, October 29.

——. 2001. *Outdoor News Bulletin.* Washington, D.C.: Wildlife Management Institute, January 15.

McDaniel, R. Andrew. 1996. *The National Parks on a Business Basis: Steve Mather and the National Park Service.* Working Paper 1996–1998, Political Economy Research Center, Bozeman, Montana.

McKetta, Charles, and Eric Weiner. 1994. *Socio-Economic Implications of a Below Cost Timber Program on the Wallowa-Whitman National Forest.* Moscow, ID: McKetta & Associates.

Missoulian. 2000. October 15. Missoula, MT.

Montana Department of Natural Resources and Conservation (MDNRC). 2006. *Montana Forestry Best Management Practices Monitoring: 2006 Forestry BMP Audit Report.* Missoula, MT.

Moonlight Basin. 2006. Committed to the Environment. Big Sky, MT: Moonlight Basin. Online: http://www.moonlightbasin.com/home/about/environment.html (cited February 7, 2006).

National Association of State Park Directors (NASPD). 2000. *The 2000 Annual Information Exchange.* Tucson, AZ.

——. 2002. *The 2002 Annual Information Exchange.* Tucson, AZ.

National Audubon Society (NAS). 1986. *Audubon Wildlife Report 1986.* New York.

——. 1987. *Audubon Wildlife Report 1987.* New York.

——. 2001. Audubon's Early Bird Action Agenda: Legislative Issues for the 107th Congress. http://www.audubon.org/campaign/lookout.html (cited January 9, 2008).

National Interagency Fire Center. 2000. *Site Report.* September 5. Online: http://www.nifc.gov/news/sitreprt.html (cited September 5, 2000).

National Park Service (NPS). 1991. *The National Parks: Shaping the System*. Washington, D.C.: USDI.
———. 1999–2002. *NPS Budget Request*. Washington, D.C.: USDI.
———. 2000. *NPS Accountability Report Fiscal Year 2000*. Washington, D.C.: USDI.
———. 2003. *NPS Budget Justifications*. Washington, D.C.: USDI.
———. 2009. *The Fiscal Year 2009 Greenbook*. Washington, D.C.: USDI.
Nelson, Robert H. 1994–95. Transferring Federal Lands in the West to the States: How Would it Work? *Points West Chronicle*, Winter.
———. 1994. Government as Theater: Toward a New Paradigm for the Public Lands. *University of Colorado Law Review* 65: 335–368.
———. 1995. *Public Lands and Private Rights: The Failure of Scientific Management*. Lanham, MD: Rowman & Littlefield
———. 1999. Ending the Forest Fire Gridlock: Making Fire Fighting in the West a State and Local Responsibility. *Environmental Studies Program*. Washington, D.C.: Competitive Enterprise Institute, March.
———. 2000. *A Burning Issue*. Lanham, MD: Rowman & Littlefield.
New Mexico State Land Office. Various years. *Annual Report*. Santa Fe, NM.
Office of Inspector General, U.S. Department of Agriculture. 2002. Audits. Online: www.usda.gov/oig/auditsfma.htm. (cited November 21, 2002).
Office of Management and Budget (OMB). 1999. *Budget of the U.S. Government Fiscal Year 2000*. Online: www.access.gpo.gov/usbudget/fy2000/other.html (cited January 5, 2000).
———. 2003. *Budget of the United States government, FY 2003*, Public Budget Database. Online: www.whitehouse.gov/omb/budget/fy2003/db.html (cited May 20, 2002).
———. 2008. *ExpectMore.gov*. Public National Park Service—Natural Resource Stewardship. Online: http://www.whitehouse.gov/omb/expectmore/summary/10001089.2003.html (cited May 22, 2008).
Olson, Steven D. 1996. The Historical Occurrence of Fire in Central Hardwoods, with Emphasis on South Central Indiana. *Natural Areas Journal* 16(3): 248–256.
Oregonian. 2001. November 15.
O'Toole, Randal. 1988. *Reforming the Forest Service*. Washington, D.C.: Island Press.
———. 1997. Should Congress Transfer Federal Lands to the States? *Cato Policy Analysis* No. 276, July 3. Washington, D.C.
———. 1998. #32: *Analysis of the Proposed 1999 Forest Service Budget*. Subsidies Anonymous. Oak Grove, OR: Thoreau Institute.
———. 2000. #39: *Forest Service 2001 Budget*. Subsidies Anonymous. Oak Grove, OR: Thoreau Institute.
Parker, Dominic. 2005. Conservation Easements: A Closer Look at Federal Tax Policy. *PERC Policy Series* PS-34. Bozeman, MT: Property and Environment Research Center, October.
Peterson, Jim. 1992. Grey Ghosts in the Blue Mountains. *Evergreen Magazine*, January/February.
———. 2000. Why the West's Forests are Burning Up. *Evergreen Magazine*. Winter.

Pinchot, Gifford. 1905. *Use Book*. Washington, D.C.: U.S. GPO. Online: www.lib
.duke.edu/forest/usfscoll/001-003.htm (cited May 24, 2000).

Public Employees for Environmental Responsibility (PEER). 2005. *Politics Trumps
Science at U.S. Fish & Wildlife Service*. Online: www.peer.org/news/print_detail
.php?row_id=474 (cited May 10, 2006).

Pyne, Stephen J. 2001. *Fire: A Brief History*. Seattle, WA: University of Washington
Press.

Ridenour, James M. 1994. *The National Parks Compromised*. Merrillville, Indiana:
ICS Books, Inc.

Rocky Mountain Elk Foundation. 2000. *Conservation Activities*. Online: www.rmef
.org/projects.htm (cited April 17, 2000).

San Diego Earth Times. 1999. *Sierra Club Calls Clinton's Investment in America's
Heritage a Bold Step Forward*. February. Online: http://www.sdearthtimes.com/
et0299/et0299s7.html (cited June 12, 2006).

Satchell, Michael. 1999. Parks in Peril. In *Parks for Tomorrow*. New York, NY:
Natural Resources Defense Council, Summer/Fall.

Sellars, Richard West. 1997. *Preserving Nature in the National Parks: A History*.
New Haven, CT: University Press.

Sohngen, Brent, Robert Mendelsohn, and Roger Sedjo. 1999. Forest Management,
Conservation, and Global Timber Markets. *American Journal of Agricultural Economics* (February): 1–13.

Souder. Jon A., and Sally K. Fairfax. 1996. *State Trust Lands: History, Management,
and Sustainable Use*. Lawrence, KA: University Press of Kansas.

Steen, Harold K. 1976. *The US Forest Service: A History*. Seattle, WA: University
of Washington Press.

Stegner, Wallace. 1960. Wilderness Letter. Written to the Outdoor Recreation
Resources Review Commission. Online: http://www.wilderness.org/OurIssues/
Wilderness/wildernessletter.cfm (cited January 21, 2004).

Stroup, Richard L., and Sandra L. Goodman. 1992. Property Rights, Environmental Resources, and the Future. *Harvard Journal of Law & Public Policy* 15(2): 427–454.

Tschida, Ron. 2004. Ag Program Helping Stave Off Urban Sprawl. *Bozeman Daily
Chronicle*. February 2.

Thomas, Jack Ward, Jerry F. Franklin, John Gordon, and K. Norman Johnson. 2006.
The Northwest Forest Plan: Origins, Components, Implementation Experience, and
Suggestions for Change. *Conservation Biology*. 20:(2), 277–287.

Troendle, C. A., M. S. Wilcox, and G. S. Bevenger. 1998. *The Coon Creek Water Yield
Augmentation Pilot Project*. Fort Collins, CO: Rocky Mountain Research Station.

Turner, Frederick Jackson. |1893| 1963. *The Significance of the Frontier in American
History*. Reprinted in *The Making of American History*, ed. Donald Sheehan. New
York: Hold, Rinehart & Winston.

USA Today. 1997. December 15.

U.S. Army Corps of Engineers. 2000. *Corps Facts*. February 1. Online www.hq.usace
.army.mil/cepa/pubs/cf-missions.htm (cited March 8, 2000).

U.S. Congress, Senate, Committee on Interior and Insular Affairs. *A University
View of the Forest Service*. [Prepared by a Select Committee of the University

of Montana at the Request of Senator Metcalf, known as the "Bolle Report."]
S.Doc. No. 91-115. 91st Congress, 2d Session. Washington, D.C.: U.S. Govt.
Print. Off., Dec. 1, 1970.

U.S. Department of Agriculture (USDA), office of Inspector General Western Region. 2006. *Audit Report: Forest Service Large Fire Suppression Costs.* Report No.
08601-44-SF. Washington, D.C., November.

U.S. Department of the Interior (USDI). 1992. *Inspector General's Report on Land
Acquisitions,* —36974, 100 I.D. 195. Washington, D.C.: Office of Inspector General, July 30.

———. 1999. *Audit Report: Land Acquisition Activities, National Park Service.* Report No. 99-I-518. Washington, D.C.: Office of Inspector General, May.

———. 2002. U.S. Fish and Wildlife Service Awards $68 Million in Grants to 16
States for Endangered Species Habitat Conservation Planning and Habitat Acquisition Projects. News Release. Office of the Secretary, Office of Intergovernmental
and External Affairs, Washington, D.C., September 13.

———. 2007. *National Policy Issuance #99-01. Subject: Mission Statement.* Online:
http://www.fws.gov/policy/npi99_01.html (cited December 30, 2008).

———. 2008. Endanagered Species Program. Endangered Species Permits. HCPs in
Development. *NiSource Habitat Conservation Plan.* Online: http://www.fws.gov/
midwest/Endangered/permits/hcp/nisource/index.html (cited December 30, 2008).

U.S. Department of Interior (USDI) and U.S. Department of Agriculture (USDA
and USDI). 2001. *Recreational Fee Demonstration Program: Progress Report to
Congress, Fiscal Year 2000.* Washington, D.C.

———. 2002. *Recreation Fee Demonstration Program Report to Congress Fiscal
Year 2001.* April 15.

Vincent, Carol Hardy, and David Whiteman. 2002. *National Park Management
and Recreation.* Congressional Research Service. Washington, D.C. Order Code
IB10093. Updated October 25. Online: http://www.ncseonline.org/NLE/CRSreports/
Nov02/IB10093.pdf. (cited December 30, 2008).

Wagner, Eric. 1998. Favorable Conditions of Water Flows. *Colorado West News
Magazine,* Spring: 5–7.

Wall Street Journal. 1999. November 12.

Washington Department of Natural Resources. Various years. *Annual Report.* Olympia.

Western Communities for Safe and Healthy Forests (WCSHF). 1997. *Media Resource Guide: The Lake Tahoe Presidential Event.* Sacramento, CA.

Wilderness Society (WS), et al. 2002. *Fiscal Year 2003 Recommendations for Funding
America's Public Lands* Online: http://216.197.110.2/Library/Documents/loader
.cfm?url=/commonspot/security/getfile.cfm&PageID=3050 (cited April 3, 2003).

Wildlife Conservation Fund of America (WCFA). 2001. *2001 Survey of State Wildlife
Agency Revenue.* Columbus, OH: WCFA.

Wilkinson, Todd. 1998. *Science under Siege.* Boulder, CO: Johnson Printing.

Wyoming Board of Land Commissioners. Various years. *Annual Report.* Cheyenne.

Zinn, Jeffrey. 1998. Land and Water Conservation Fund: Current Status and Issues.
Congressional Research Service Report for Congress, #97–792. Washington, D.C.

Index

147

About the Author

Holly Fretwell is an adjunct instructor at Montana State University teaching sections of the Economic Way of Thinking, Principles of Microeconomics, Natural Resource Economics, and Economics and the Environment. She is a research fellow at the Property and Environment Research Center, where she continues to analyze the implications of federal land policy and environmental stewardship. As author and co-author of numerous articles on natural resource issues, Fretwell has been published in professional journals and the popular press including the *Wall Street Journal, Journal for Environmental Economics and Management, Duke Environmental Law and Policy Forum, Journal of Forestry,* and *Consumer's Research.* She has presented papers promoting the use of markets in public land management and has provided congressional testimony on the state of U.S. national parks and the future of the Forest Service. She has also recently published a children's book on climate change, *The Sky's Not Falling: Why It's OK to Chill About Global Warming* (World Ahead Publishing 2007), to help encourage parents, teachers, and kids to become critical thinkers. Fretwell holds a bachelor's degree in political science and a master's degree in resource economics from Montana State University. She resides in Montana where she can continually enjoy the great outdoors.

CPSIA information can be obtained
at www.ICGtesting.com
Printed in the USA
LVHW091344290819
629400LV00001B/20/P